Situational Game Design

Brian Upton

CRC Press

Taylor & Francis Group
Boca Raton London New York

CRC Press is an imprint of the
Taylor & Francis Group, an **informa** business

AN A K PETERS BOOK

CRC Press
Taylor & Francis Group
6000 Broken Sound Parkway NW, Suite 300
Boca Raton, FL 33487-2742

CRC Press is an imprint of Taylor & Francis Group, an Informa business

No claim to original U.S. Government works

Printed on acid-free paper

International Standard Book Number-13: 978-1-138-03181-4 (paperback)
International Standard Book Number-13: 978-1-138-30518-2 (hardback)

This book contains information obtained from authentic and highly regarded sources. Reasonable efforts have been made to publish reliable data and information, but the author and publisher cannot assume responsibility for the validity of all materials or the consequences of their use. The authors and publishers have attempted to trace the copyright holders of all material reproduced in this publication and apologize to copyright holders if permission to publish in this form has not been obtained. If any copyright material has not been acknowledged please write and let us know so we may rectify in any future reprint.

Library of Congress Cataloging-in-Publication Data

Names: Upton, Brian, 1964- author.
Title: Situational game design / Brian Upton.
Description: Boca Raton, FL : Taylor & Francis, CRC Press, 2018.
Identifiers: LCCN 2017021955| ISBN 9781138031814 (pbk. : alk. paper) | ISBN 9781138305182 (hardback : alk. paper)
Subjects: LCSH: Video games--Authorship. | Computer games--Design. | Games--Psychological aspects. | Game theory. | Situation (Philosophy)
Classification: LCC GV1469.34.A97 U68 2018 | DDC 794.8/1536--dc23
LC record available at https://lccn.loc.gov/2017021955

Visit the Taylor & Francis Web site at
http://www.taylorandfrancis.com

and the CRC Press Web site at
http://www.crcpress.com

Printed and bound in the United States of America by
Edwards Brothers Malloy on sustainably sourced paper

Contents

Acknowledgments

I'D LIKE TO THANK Brenda Romero for providing the impetus for this project.

I'd also like to thank the helpful staff of the Starbucks at Olympic and Westwood in Los Angeles, where most of this book was written.

But most of all, I'd like to thank my wife and interlocutor, Elizabeth Randell Upton. The ideas contained within this book are the result of hundreds of hours of conversation between us. Without her collaboration, this book would not exist.

Author

Brian Upton is a freelance game design consultant. A 20-year veteran of the game industry, he was one of the founders of Red Storm Entertainment, where he designed the original *Rainbow Six* and *Ghost Recon*. From 2002 to 2016, he was a senior game designer at Sony's Santa Monica Studio, where he collaborated with external teams bringing innovative indie titles to the PlayStation.

He has served on the advisory boards of game design programs at University of California, Santa Cruz, New York University, and University of Limerick. He is a regular speaker at conferences such as Game Developers Conference, Games for Change, and Digital Dragons. His previous book, *The Aesthetic of Play* (MIT Press 2015), explored the relationship between games, stories, and meaning.

CHAPTER 1

Introduction

G AMES ARE INTERACTIVE. THERE'S a give-and-take to playing a game that isn't present when we read a novel or watch a movie or listen to a piece of music. We make a move, and our opponent (or the game itself) responds, and that response affects which moves we make in the future. The outcome of a novel is predetermined; we can't change how it ends. But the outcome of a game remains in question right up until the final move, and the moves we make along the way determine what that outcome will be.

Because interactivity is so central to games, it's not surprising that a great deal of game design theory is focused on how to design good interactions. How do you structure your mechanics to create a feeling of agency? How do you write rules that offer challenging choices? How do you provide meaningful feedback? How do you create a satisfying sense of progression and accomplishment? These are all important design questions, and they're all grounded in the notion that it is primarily the quality of a game's interactions that determines its worth as a play experience.

However, while interaction may be fundamental to games, games are more than just interaction. We know this because many games feel playful even when we aren't interacting with them. The most obvious example is chess. In a game of chess, there are often long intervals between moves. And yet, even though our interactions are sporadic, our feeling of play is continuous. Playing chess doesn't consist of long stretches of boredom punctuated by occasional flurries of playfulness. Rather, a sustained feeling of playfulness spans the intervals between our interactions. Making moves is an essential part of the experience of playing chess, but if we want to understand how it feels to play chess, we also need to understand how play unfolds when we're not moving. We need to understand non-interactive play.

Non-interactive play is easy to observe in turn-based games, but it shows up in other types of games as well. For example, in a puzzle game like *The Witness*, we may spend several minutes holding still and thinking. When we finally do interact with the game, it's merely to test our solution to see if it's correct. The play value of the puzzles in *The Witness* lies not just in the interactions they afford, but also in the opportunities for rumination they present.

A stealth game like *Metal Gear Solid* (*MGS*) offers similar opportunities for non-interactive play. Sometimes, the best tactic in *MGS* is to watch and wait—watch to learn the patterns of the guards, wait for the right moment to run or attack. These intervals of watching and waiting aren't boring—they're often the most intense and rewarding parts of the game. Combat, when it does occur, is less a game in its own right, and more a way of validating our choices during the non-interactive stealth game that preceded it.

Horror games offer many of the same non-interactive design challenges as stealth games. The play of a horror game exists largely in our imaginations. What makes a game scary is less a matter of what it does to us, and more a matter of our anticipation of what it might do. The interactivity of the horror game *P.T.* is limited to opening doors, walking, and looking. We have control over the pace and order that events unfold, but we're unable to change the overall flow or outcome of the experience. Indeed, it is the very inevitability of our doom that makes the game effective. We know that awful things lie ahead in *P.T.*'s claustrophobic hallways, but, horrifyingly, we lack the agency to avoid them.

Even games that seem action-packed often contain fleeting bursts of non-interactive play. We hesitate for a moment in the corridor of a first-person shooter, considering which enemies might lie around the next corner. We use a long section of straight track in a racing game to prepare for the hairpin turn we can see approaching. We linger at a safe spot in a platform, estimating the timing and risk of our next series of jumps. The fun of these games comes not just from the moments when we act, but from the moments of stillness that proceed them.

We can draw an analogy between interactivity in games and the cut in cinema. Cuts allow a cinematographer to do things that a theatrical director can't. Images can be juxtaposed in meaningful ways; the narrative can leap backward or forward in time, allowing the audience to imagine what must have happened during the missing interval. The cut is a powerful aesthetic tool and a fundamental, defining characteristic of film as an art form.

But, films are more than just sequences of cuts. The cut is a thing that a film *can* do, but it's not a thing that a film *must* do. A film doesn't cease being a film during a long continuous shot. The quality of a film isn't determined by how many cuts it contains. The cuts in a film are strategically deployed to produce particular effects; they're not sprinkled around at random just to keep the film from feeling like a stage play.

So it is with interactivity in games. Interactivity is a thing that a game *can* do, but it's not a thing that a game *must* do. A game doesn't cease being a game if it contains long stretches where the player doesn't interact. The amount of interactivity in a game doesn't determine how good it is. Interactivity is a powerful tool that can be strategically deployed within a game to produce particular aesthetic effects, but it's not the entirety of the play experience. Sometimes, the most playful thing a game can do is hold still.

THE PROBLEM WITH WINNING

There's another way that games differ from other forms of entertainment: games are winnable. The rules of a game specify an arbitrary goal that we're supposed to try to reach, and, as the game unfolds, our moves are made with that goal in mind. Good moves carry us closer to victory, and bad moves carry us further away.

This is true whether the game is competitive, cooperative, or a solo experience. Sometimes, we may work together to try to accomplish a single, shared goal, and other times we may have different goals and work in opposition to each other. But regardless of whether we are competing or collaborating, our moves are always directed toward satisfying the arbitrary win condition set out in the rules.

Books and movies and music aren't like that. There's no way to win a novel. When we watch a movie, we're not trying to work toward some specific ending. When we listen to a piece of music, we're not thinking about how to defeat our fellow audience members. Partially, this is because these mediums aren't interactive. Even if we decide that we want a movie to end in a particular way, there's no way for us to make that happen.

But, while winning and interactivity are related to each other, they're not inseparable. It's possible to have one without the other. A toy like a ball is very interactive—there are lots of different ways to play with it—but it doesn't have a built-in win condition. There's nothing inherent in a ball that makes bouncing it a "good move" and throwing it a "bad move." If we want to build a game around a ball, we need to create other rules that impose a win condition on its free-form interactivity.

Furthermore, some books *are* winnable. Murder mysteries are books, but they're also puzzles. You win a murder mystery by solving the crime before the detective does. The novel isn't interactive—you can't change how it ends. But it does present you with a goal and the opportunity to work toward it. The pieces you move when you read a murder mystery aren't pieces on a board, they're pieces in your mind—suspects and suppositions and hypotheses. You're trying to figure out an arrangement for these mental pieces that fits within the evidence of text. A murder mystery is winnable without being interactive.

Just as with interactivity, giving the player a way to win is a thing that a game *can* do, but it's not a thing that a game *must* do. A game doesn't cease being a game if it's unwinnable. How difficult it is to win a game doesn't determine how good it is. Winning is a tool that can be deployed within a game to produce particular aesthetic effects, but it's not essential for a game to feel playful.

The most obvious example of this are tabletop role-playing games like *Dungeons and Dragons (D&D)*. The rules of *D&D* contain a number of explicit goals. Players are expected to stay alive, to accumulate treasure, to level up their characters—and these goals structure how much of the gameplay unfolds. Players try to make moves that maximize their success within this framework—they try to employ the most powerful attacks, discover the biggest caches of loot, seek out the most challenging monsters. Good moves are moves that carry them closer to these win conditions, and bad moves are moves that carry them further away.

But, sometimes, players deliberately choose losing moves. A player may charge into near-certain doom because they're playing a Lawful Good paladin who has sworn to protect the weak. A player may throw away a rare spell book because they're playing an illiterate barbarian who doesn't know how valuable it is. In addition to the explicit goals expressed in the game's rules, players possess a set of intrinsic motivations derived from their sense of narrative, character, and situation. And these intrinsic motivations also shape their trajectory through the play space.

So, play is more than just winning. Sometimes, play is performance—it's trying on different identities or creatively expressing your own personality.

Sometimes, play is exploration—it's poking around in odd nooks and crannies and experiencing the thrill of the unexpected. Sometimes, play is destruction—it's deliberately smashing things just to watch them fly to pieces. Sometimes, play is camaraderie—it's experiencing a sense of belonging with a team or a community.

All of these intrinsic motivations are present in every game, although often they can be suppressed if the game has strong enough win conditions. Just as anticipatory and interpretive play demand a degree of stillness, so performative and exploratory play demand a degree of aimlessness. If the player constantly feels pressure to move toward victory—if there's always a new enemy to defeat or a new challenge to overcome—then there's no room left for the elaborated imaginative riffs that characterize a good session of make-believe.

WHAT IS SITUATIONAL GAME DESIGN?

Situational game design is a design methodology that takes into account how play unfolds when the player either isn't interacting or isn't trying to win. It sees interactivity and winning not as foundational to play, but merely as two useful strategies for the construction of playful situations.

Most approaches to game design are *transactional*. They treat games as self-contained systems that stand apart from the player who is playing them. Playfulness exists at the interface between player and game. It emerges from the moves the game allows the player to make toward winning, and from the countermoves the game makes in response (Figure 1.1). If the player doesn't interact with the game, or if they're not trying to win, they're not playing.

Seen from this perspective, game design is about creating self-contained systems that offer clear goals, interesting moves, and useful feedback. Transactional design is *game-centric*. The player is abstracted away and the game is considered in isolation. With the player out of the picture, the game's quality is determined entirely by its formal system. Different players may play the game well or poorly, but the game itself is always the

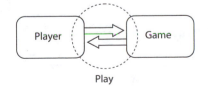

Play

FIGURE 1.1   Transactional design.

same. It always offers the same challenges and the same opportunities for action regardless of who is playing it.

Situational design is different. It's a *player-centric* approach to design rather than a game-centric one. Instead of focusing on the *actions* the player can perform, it focuses on the *situations* the player can encounter. Some of these situations may invite interaction, but just as often they may invite anticipation, or interpretation, or introspection, and all of these ways to play contribute in their own way to the overall texture of the experience. Instead of assuming that all of the player's actions are directed toward winning, it recognizes the existence of a range of other motivations and provides a framework for analyzing how the game's mechanics support these other goals.

In situational design, the nexus of play lies not in the interface between the player and the game, but inside the player's mind (Figure 1.2). Some of the moves the player makes will affect the external state of the game, but others will affect their internal understanding of the game, or even their understanding of themselves and the world at large. The game's system has been expanded so that it is no longer coterminous with the game's formal rules. It also includes the attitudes, personal history, and intrinsic motivations that the player contributes to the experience. What this means is that even if different players are presented with exactly the same rules, they will nevertheless wind up playing different games. This is not because the game adapts itself to its players, but because the play space that each player occupies is determined by their individual knowledge and intent.

In situational design, play is *embodied*. Games are not playful in and of themselves. They only become playful when they intersect with a receptive player. Furthermore, there are no universal players. Each game has its own *assumed player* who completes it and makes it playful. Different games can be completed in different ways, and consequentially have different assumed players. If we want to understand how a game plays, it's not enough to study its rules in isolation. We need to take

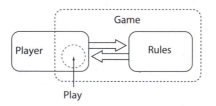

FIGURE 1.2   Situational design.

into account how its assumed player completes its system, and how the distance between the game's actual players and its assumed player can cause that system to break down.

By focusing on the player's experience and not the game's structure, situational design gives us a way to analyze how play unfolds during moments of both stillness and aimlessness. If play is something that happens inside the player's head, then we don't need to design systems that keep the player constantly busy. We can deliberately craft intervals where the game holds still, giving the player room to mull over the implications and ramifications of their situation. Or we can deliberately create play spaces that don't have any explicit goals, secure in the knowledge that the player's own intrinsic motivations will carry them forward.

MAKING MEANING WITH GAMES

The biggest advantage of situational game design, however, is that it provides an explanation for how games make meaning. We know that games can make meaning because some games change us when we play them. A trace of the experience lingers after the game is over—a new idea, a new emotion, a new way of understanding the world, a new way of understanding ourselves. We're different people than we were before we encountered them. So the question isn't whether games can be meaningful. The question is how this meaning-making occurs, and how we should go about designing games to make it likely to occur. And situational design gives us a way to answer both these questions.

The standard way to understand meaning-making is semiotics. Semiotics is grounded in a transmission model of communication. The speaker encodes the concept or feeling they want to convey (the signified) with an arbitrary symbol (the signifier). The signifier is then transmitted to the listener who decodes it to recover the intended meaning. There are, of course, many complications and elaborations to this basic model, but the foundational structure remains the same: Meaning is produced by the flow of signifiers from speaker to listener, and if we want to make an experience feel meaningful then we need to pay close attention to which signifiers we're transmitting.

This transmission model works well enough for deterministic media like books and movies. The sequential words in a novel can be analyzed as a stream of signifiers, each one transmitting a little bit of meaning from the author to the reader. The meaning that lingers after the reader has finished arises from a "piling up" of all the individual signifiers that were transmitted during the course of the reading. We can thus identify particular images or symbols in the text and link them to particular thoughts or feeling that the reader experiences.

But the standard semiotic model breaks down when we to get at the heart of how meaning-making operates in games. Much of the meaning that we take away from a game is not a function of the signifiers that it transmits to us, but rather of the things it allows us to do. Games don't tell us things; they allow us to perform things. And that performance is where much of the meaning of a game lies.

If we analyze a game, we can sometimes identify images or symbols that function as signifiers in the standard semiotic sense—a stop sign in a game means much the same thing as a stop sign in a movie. But if we try to pin down the particular signifier that transmits the feeling of companionship that we experience when we play *Journey*, for example, we discover we can't, even though that feeling of companionship lies at the heart of what *Journey* means. *Journey*'s meaning-making is not explainable through the standard semiotic model because most of its meaning doesn't arise from a transmission of signifiers.

By situating play in the mind of the player, situational design provides a new formalism for understanding how meaning emerges from an aesthetic experience. Rather than meaning being seen as something that's transmitted, it's seen as something that's constructed. Some of a player's moves change the external state of the game, but other moves change their internal understanding of the game, and the effects of these internally directed moves can linger after the external game ends.

A game doesn't transmit its meaning to a player in a stream of encoded signifiers. Rather, the game's rules intersect with the player's understanding to structure a sequence of situations, and how the player responds to these situations in turn alters the player's understanding. This shift in understanding in response to the contingencies of playful situations is where the meaning-making power of a game resides.

So, the meaning of a game emerges from an accumulation of strategies. These strategies are a response to the structure of the game, not a recapitulation of it. *Journey* doesn't contain "companionship" anywhere within itself. It doesn't transmit "companionship" to the player through a coded signifier. Rather, it structures a space in which a move toward companionship is an effective strategy, and so after the game ends a lingering trace of that tendency toward companionship remains behind in the mind of the player.

The notion that players invent strategies in response to the challenges presented by games is nothing new, of course. But since most games are designed along transactional lines, these strategies tend to be limited to effective ways to win. If you treat a game as a self-contained system, then the strategies you develop in response to it will tend to be meaningful only within that system. Getting good at *League of Legends* may have some spillover into your day-to-day life, but most of the strategies you learn from playing it will only be meaningful in the context of it or similar games.

The power of situational design (from the perspective of making games meaningful) is that it encourages the designer to treat the player's pre-existing attitudes and feelings as part of the game system. As a result, a game can be structured around situations where the "best move" is not necessarily one that advances the player toward an arbitrary win state, but rather one that shifts the player's attitudes or feelings in satisfying ways. Such moves are more likely to have a lingering effect on the player, to be more personally significant than simply learning how to operate effectively within the walled garden of the transactional game.

In other words, if we design game systems to make use of a player's existing attitudes toward the world, then the strategies they adopt as they play the game will affect those attitudes. The game changes the player, not because it tells the player something new, but because it gives the player a space to inhabit in which a new way of being is an effective strategy.

SUMMARY

Situational design is a player-centric approach to game design and analysis. It takes into account not just the rules of the game, but the attitude of the player toward the game and the context of how the game is played. As a result, it's able to address design questions that transactional design normally overlooks.

Specifically, situational design is good for analyzing non-interactive play—the moments during a game when the player is engaged in either anticipation or interpretation instead of interaction. It's also good for analyzing non-goal-directed play—the moments during a game when the player stops trying to win and instead pursues some other objective such as performance or identity construction.

But, situational design is also good for analyzing how games make meaning. It's a tool for getting at how the moves we make during a game translate into the significance that we ascribe to the experience of playing. It provides an alternative to traditional semiotics—rather than seeing meaning as something that is transmitted from work to audience, situational design treats it as something that is constructed by the audience in response to the demands of the work.

CHAPTER 2

Situations, Constraints, and Moves

THE CORE CONCEPT OF situational game design is (unsurprisingly) the *situation*. A situation is an interval of play that contains a choice. The simplest example of a situation is a turn in a turn-based game. You roll the dice in *Monopoly* and move your piece. If you land on an unowned property, you must decide whether to buy it or put it up for auction. The game gives you a choice, and that choice defines a situation within the experience of playing *Monopoly*.

Situations are easier to see in turn-based games, but they occur in non-turn-based games as well. A platforming game like *Super Mario Bros.* unfolds continuously, but within its continuous flow there are moments where your opportunities to act are well defined. When you're standing on a platform, there are a limited number of places you can jump. So standing on a platform in *Super Mario Bros.* is a situation. It's an interval of play that contains a choice.

A turn in *Monopoly*, a platform in *Super Mario Bros.*, the view from a doorway in *DOOM*, a stretch of track in *Gran Turismo*, a board position in *Tetris*—all of these are situations. In each case, the game offers us a range of possible actions, and provides us with time (albeit sometimes just a brief fraction of a second) to choose between them.

We can conceptualize any play experience as a chain of situations. Within each situation we have a choice of moves, and the move we choose determines our next situation. These situations are both embodied and temporal—they are not part of the game's static structure. Rather, they are a description of how the game dynamically unfolds in real time as we play it.

The notion of the situation gives us a way to break down the experience of playing a game into small, manageable chunks. It allows us to analyze the player's behavior and motivation from moment to moment, taking into account how it shifts and flows in response to how the game unfolds. This fine-grain analysis allows us to pick apart the many different types of play a player experiences, and understand how each contributes to the overall texture of the experience.

CONSTRAINTS

Situations are structured by *constraints*. When we're within a situation we're offered a range of moves to choose from. The constraints that structure a situation determine which moves we're allowed to make, and therefore what choices it offers us.

The most obvious type of constraint is a *rule*. A rule is formal declaration of what is (or isn't) allowed within a game. The rules of a game may be printed on a piece of paper or shared verbally between players or encoded in software, but however they're expressed, they form a rigid system of constraints that limit our opportunities to act.

For example, the rules of chess state that pawns can only move forward; they can't move backward or side to side. If you're playing chess, you can't pick up a pawn and place it anywhere you want; you can only place it on one of the squares that the rules permit. Playing chess is a matter of submitting to the authority of this rule (and many other rules besides) and restricting your actions accordingly. The situations we encounter in chess are determined by how its various rules work together to constrain our choices.

Video games have rules just like board games. When we play them, there are specific things that we are either required, or forbidden to do. However, there are many other things in video games that constrain our actions besides explicit rules. For example, if you're racing to claim the point in *Overwatch*, your actions are also limited by the geometry of the level and the actions of the other players. Because there's a wall ahead, you can only run left or right—you can't run straight ahead. Because there's an enemy guarding the main approach, you need to take an alternative route to the objective.

So rules aren't the only type of constraint. Depending on the game, there can be many other things that can affect our opportunities to act. We can be constrained by level layout, or by enemy behavior, or by real-world physics, or by social convention, or by our sense of performing a role, or by our own strategies. Anything that privileges one line of action over another is a constraint.

The power of thinking in terms of constraints rather than rules is that it allows us to put all the various aspects of a game that affect our moment-to-moment actions on the same footing. Rather than focusing our attention exclusively on the game's formal structure, constraints allow us to see how that formal structure combines with other restrictions and affordances to generate the actual experience of playing the game.

Consider baseball. The way the ball flies through the air, the way it bounces on the ground, the way it ricochets off a bat—all of these things affect how the game unfolds, and the situations that it offers its players. There are things baseball players don't do, not because they're forbidden by the rules, but because they're physically impossible. Physics matters to how baseball plays.

So the situations that we encounter during a game of baseball are structured by a hybrid system of constraints. Some of these constraints are official rules that we voluntarily adhere to, while others are the non-negotiable physical properties of the field, the equipment, and the players' bodies. In fact, the rules of baseball have been designed with these physical constraints in mind. The strike zone is sized to accommodate these physical constraints. If human arms were stronger, if human reflexes were slower, if the field were twice as large, if the ball were half as heavy, then the strike zone would need to be resized to keep the game fair.

Games that rely heavily on physical constraints are usually called "sports." Baseball, soccer, weight lifting, swimming, cycling, archery, curling—all of these ways to play are structured by the real-world properties of human bodies and physical objects. But even games that aren't as physically determined as sports are can have physical constraints. Playing a video game with a controller is a different experience than playing it with a mouse and keyboard. What we can do in a video game is partially determined by the physicality of our input device—by the layout of its buttons and triggers, by the way our fingers must bend to provide the necessary inputs. There is a gap between what the game programmatically allows, and what our bodies can physically accomplish, and that gap constrains how we play. (The existence of this gap is explicitly recognized by speedrunners who distinguish between "unassisted" and "tool-assisted" runs—between playthroughs that are constrained by the physicality of a controller held by human hands, and those that use scripting or slow motion to bypass those constraints.)

There are other kinds of constraints besides the formal and the physical. Sometimes, we avoid doing things in a game not because they're against the rules or physically impossible, but because they're socially unacceptable. If the game is supposed to be friendly, we might avoid making moves that are too brutal or cutthroat. We may even bend the rules a little, allowing mulligans or do-overs to keep things convivial. Even if we're playing competitively, certain moves or tactics may be avoided because they seem unfair or cheap. For example, an easy way to run up a high score in a first-person shooter is to camp the spawn points and kill new players as they enter the game. Even if the rules of the game allow camping, social pressure may prevent us from actually engaging in it.

Sometimes, we're constrained not by our real-world social obligations, but by the fictional role we've adopted within the game. In a tabletop role-playing game, players may avoid certain moves not because the rules forbid them, but because they're out of character. A heroic knight may refuse to run from an unwinnable fight because dishonor is worse than death. The fact that running away is allowed by the rules is immaterial. All the situations the player encounters within their role-playing experience will be structured by this performative constraint; running away doesn't exist as a meaningful move for the player to make.

We can also be constrained by our expertise. If we know a game well, there will be some moves we avoid making not because they're forbidden, but because they're foolish. Consider the opening of a game of Go. Taking symmetries into account, there are 55 possible locations where a player can place the first stone. However, experienced go players know that only about eight of these 55 locations are strategically viable, and of those eight, only three are used in most professional matches: the 3–3 point, the 3–4 point, and the 4–4 point. There's no rule against starting a game of go by placing a stone right in the center of the board, or all the way in one corner, but experienced go players don't make these moves because they know they're worthless.

Because of the role such strategic constraints play in structuring game-play situations, the play value of a game can vary widely depending on how well we understand it. Tic-tac-toe is fun until you figure out that there's a simple master strategy that guarantees a win or a draw for whoever plays first. Conversely, some games become interesting only after we learn a lot about them. Contract bridge requires players to bid on how many tricks they think their team can take. But this bidding play assumes that the players understand the game's trick-taking mechanic well enough to make a decent estimate. A complete novice won't understand the game well enough to properly bid on a contract, and so the bidding portion of the game won't feel very playful.

The first step to analyzing a situation within a gameplay experience is to understand the constraints that structure it. Which rules apply at the current moment? How does the layout of the level limit the player's actions? How does their knowledge of the game affect which moves they feel they can choose? All of these factors determine the playfulness of a situation.

MOVES

Constraints are dynamic. They shift and change over the course of the game. Every game has a large number of *potential constraints*—a large number of different ways that it can restrict our actions. But generally, only a handful of these potential constraints apply to our current situation. These are the *active constraints*—the constraints that actually determine what moves we can make right now.

For example, chess has a pawn promotion rule. If you move one of your pawns to the far end of the board, you can replace it with a more powerful piece. The pawn promotion rule is a potential constraint that can possibly affect our actions, but for most of the game it doesn't matter. It's only late in the game when the board opens up and the surviving pawns have advanced deep into enemy territory that the possibility of pawn promotion begins to significantly constrain our choice of moves. At that point, a potential constraint has become an active one.

When we're analyzing the flow of play in a game, it's important to keep the distinction between potential and active constraints in mind. The playfulness of a game is a function of its active constraints not its potential ones. When it comes to play, the static structure of a rule set isn't nearly as important as its dynamic behavior: Does the game consistently produce situations that are made interesting by the particular arrangement of their active constraints?

The notion of an active constraint gives us a way to formally define what we mean by "making a move." A move is anything the player does that changes the game's active constraints. There are many actions that we can perform during a game that aren't moves: double-checking the cards in our hand, tallying up our victory points, jumping in place on a platform, triggering an emote animation. Unlike these other actions, a move is an action that matters. It matters because it changes the game's active constraints, and by changing the game's active constraints, it changes our situation.

A move doesn't have to be deliberate for it to count as a move. In fact, most of the moves we make during any game are made unconsciously. We don't think to ourselves, "Hmmm ... I have a choice to make here." Rather, we simply do what we think we should, given the situation at hand. We swerve left at the fork in the road, we jump to the next platform, we pull the trigger of our gun—in each situation we clearly have made a choice, but it was not a choice we made through conscious deliberation.

Furthermore, sometimes a game's active constraints can change without us doing *anything*. In a racing game, the other cars will continue to zoom around the track even if our car is parked at the curb. In a first-person shooter, the enemies will attack us even if we don't fight back. If our active constraints can change even when we do nothing, then doing nothing is also a move.

THE GAME AS UNDERSTOOD

Different constraints are enforced in different ways. Sometimes, we enforce them upon ourselves, but other times they're imposed upon us. If you play a game of solitaire with a physical deck of cards, the only thing stopping you from peeking is your personal commitment to following the rules. But if you play the same game on a computer, the option of cheating is taken out of your hands. You don't peek, not because you've chosen not to, but because you can't; the game's programming prevents it. Similarly, if you're playing tennis, your choice of shots is partially determined by the physics of the ball and your physical abilities. You don't choose to enforce these particular constraints upon yourself; they're present whether you want them to be or not.

However, even when a constraint is imposed upon us by some external force, we generally accommodate this restriction by adopting a matching internal constraint. Once we realize the solitaire program won't let us cheat, we don't keep trying to peek. We don't swing at tennis balls that are out of our reach. As we wander the corridors of a first-person shooter, we don't bump into the walls. The game's code imposes a hard external constraint ("walls are impassible") on our actions, but that hard constraint rarely comes into play because we impose a softer internal constraint ("avoid walls") on ourselves. The internal constraint stops us before we reach the external constraint. And this internal constraint affects our actions even in situations where the external constraint doesn't apply. Some games even hide secrets behind non-collidable walls; the game's coded constraints allow passage, but our internal constraints make the secret hard to find.

This mirroring of external and internal constraints is so natural and ubiquitous that we tend to overlook it. We avoid colliding with the walls in a first-person shooter. We don't try to run through the linebacker in a game of football. We avoid picking up the ball during a refereed soccer match. We don't steal money in a game of *Monopoly*. What stops us is not the game code, or real-world physics, or the referee, or our opponents. What stops us is our internal beliefs about those things. Even when hard external constraints exist, we rarely run up against them. The unfolding of any game with external constraints is determined almost entirely by what we believe those constraints to be, rather than what they actually are.

With this in mind, we can make a useful distinction between three different aspects of any game: the Game as Designed, the Game as Experienced, and the Game as Understood (Figure 2.1).

The Game as Designed is the system of external constraints created by the designer—its written rules, its intended physicality, its programmatic embodiment. The Game as Experienced is how the designer's intent manifests itself within a particular play session—the way the game unfolds, the chain of situations that it evokes. The Game as Understood is our personal grasp of the game—our internal mental representation of its rules and its physicality, our grasp of its social context, and our sense of what strategies it requires.

These three aspects are related to each other, but they're not identical. There are always gaps. There are always situations that the rules permit that don't arise when the game is played, and there are always situations that arise when the game is played that the designer never anticipated. The players' understanding of the game is influenced by the situations they

FIGURE 2.1   Three aspects of a game.

encounter, but that understanding can diverge widely from the rules that made those situations possible.

This gap between Game as Designed and Game as Understood is particularly easy to see in video games. The rules of a video game are contained in its programming, but our understanding of those rules is not programmatic. We understand what the code does, but we don't achieve this understanding by running a copy of the code in our minds. Instead, we adopt a set of internal constraints that are *functionally equivalent* to game's programming without replicating it.

For example, artificial intelligence (AI) characters in video games programmatically "see" with line-of-sight checks. The game calculates a line that runs from a character to the thing they're trying to see, and if the line doesn't intersect any solid objects, then the thing is visible. But if we're trying to hide from a monster, we don't think, "How do I keep the monster's line-of-sight checks from succeeding?" We think, "How do I keep the monster from seeing me?"

The game's code implements a system of constraints—the line-of-sight code—that determines whether the monster attacks. But our understanding of those constraints is embodied by a completely different system of constraints that happen to be functionally equivalent. If we do things to keep the monster from seeing us (according to our internal mental constraints) then it's likely that the monster's line-of-sight checks will fail (according to the game's external programmatic constraints).

But while it's likely that our actions will cause the game's line-of-sight checks to fail, such an outcome isn't guaranteed. In the real world, seeing involves more than just tracing a line from your head to your target. It depends on light and shadow and fog and translucency and contrast and camouflage. And since line-of-sight checks are computationally expensive, the game might not perform them every frame, or it might only check to see if your torso is visible, ignoring your limbs and head. As a result, there will always be cases in a video game where you believe that you're hidden and you're not, or you believe that you're not hidden and you are. There's always a gap between the external programmatic rule and the player's internal non-programmatic understanding of it, between Game as Designed and Game as Understood.

This gap between a player's understanding and programmatic reality crops up everywhere in video games. When one character "hits" another in a fighting game, the game doesn't calculate an actual impact, only the intersection of two hitboxes. When a character becomes "angry" there is no real emotion involved with all its nuance and messiness; it's just a different state in the AI's state machine. "Darkness" isn't darkness, "injury" isn't injury, "movement" isn't movement—we don't understand these things within a video game by grasping their algorithmic implementation, but rather by adopting a different system of non-algorithmic constraints that is similar but not identical.

When the gap between our understanding and a game's programming becomes noticeably large, we call it an "exploit." Exploits are often described as holes in a game's rules—instances where some edge condition in the code allows the player to get away with something that the designer didn't intend. But if would be more accurate to say that an exploit is a hole in our understanding. The game always does exactly what its code says it should do; it only seems to have a hole because we expect it to do something different. An exploit is a moment when the algorithmic reality of a game's implementation intrudes into our functional understanding.

It might seem as though the gap between Game as Designed and Game as Understood could be eliminated with the right instructions, training, or tutorials. These techniques can certainly close the gap, but they never eliminate it entirely. This is because players are not passive blank slates. Anything that you teach the player will inevitably be filtered through their own prior knowledge, and their acquired knowledge will inevitably shift and change as they develop their own strategic constraints in response to the situations they encounter within the Game as Experienced.

As a designer, it's easy to lapse into the trap of thinking that the rules you invent will be the rules that the players will play by. But the relationship between Game as Designed and Game as Understood is far more complicated and nuanced. Every external constraint that you impose upon the player will eventually be mirrored by a corresponding internal constraint in the player's mind. But this mirroring is rarely precise. It always is mediated by the contingencies of the Game as Experienced, and the prior assumptions that the player brings to the encounter.

PRE-EXISTING CONSTRAINTS

We always bring our own pre-existing internal constraints to any game we play. These pre-existing constraints can arise from a variety of different sources. Some come from our understanding of the real world, but others come from our understanding of other games.

For example, in the real world it takes more effort to walk up a hill than to walk on level ground. Video games usually ignore this distinction, but, nevertheless, when we encounter a hill in a video game we're more likely to skirt it than climb it. Our understanding of real-world movement imposes a variety of soft pathing constraints on our traversal of a virtual space—we avoid hills, we follow paths, we resist stepping into water, we drive on the legal side of the road, and so on. These soft pathing constraints affect the situations we encounter as we play.

We also borrow constraints from other games we've played. This is true even with something as simple as board game. There are many elements of playing a board game that the rules don't bother to explain. They don't tell you what it means to "take your turn," for example. ("First you do some things while your opponent watches. Then your opponent does some things while you watch.") Or what it means to "roll the dice." ("Pick up the numbered cubes and toss them so they tumble several times before they come to rest. Read the numbers off their tops.") Most of us learn these basic game mechanics as children, and knowledge of them is so ubiquitous that board game designers can assume that that they don't need to teach them to us.

If you're designing a racing game, you can assume that many of your players will have previously played other racing games, and their understanding of those games will affect how they play your game. They will expect the controls to be laid out in a certain way, and they will expect the car to handle in a certain way, and they will make decisions according to those expectations, regardless of how your particular game actually plays. If your game differs too radically from these genre conventions it will be unplayable, not because it's a bad game when considered in isolation, but because it has failed to accommodate the pre-existing constraints that the typical player brings to the experience. The Game as (Mis)understood will obscure the actual affordances offered by the Game as Designed.

This is the power and danger of genre. A genre is a collection of constraints that players can take as a given. When you play a game from a particular genre, you don't need to learn all of its genre-specific constraints before you start to play—you already know them from having played similar games. And so play can begin immediately, without the need for instructions or a tutorial.

If you believe you're playing a horror game, you'll move through the game world differently than if you believe you're playing a first-person shooter. You'll be more cautious and apprehensive. You'll pay more attention to small details. You'll be more careful about opening doors or turning corners. Part of what makes a horror game scary is our knowledge that it's supposed to be scary, and that knowledge causes us to engage with it in ways that magnify our fear. Our genre expectations form part of the system of constraints that we use to play the game.

Often, learning a game is not a matter of memorizing its rules, but of noticing cues that suggest which of our pre-existing constraints we should adopt as we play. It's not a coincidence that virtual game spaces often mimic real-world spaces. They do so not because there is something inherently playful about the real world, but because such mimicry encourages us to use our knowledge of the real world as part of our system of internal constraints. We already know about trees, mountains, rivers, airplanes, cars, corridors, doorways, flashlights, guns—and so when we encounter one of these things in a game we already have a good sense of what constraints will govern our interactions with it. The line-of-sight checks performed by AI characters are designed so that our real-world knowledge of how eyesight works will be a useful constraint.

Games that take this mimicry to extremes are called "simulations," and it's interesting to note what these simulations are simulating. Even the most hard-core simulation doesn't attempt to simulate all the low-level nuances of reality—the virtual dirt below our virtual feet doesn't contain virtual earthworms made of virtual molecules. Rather, the aspects of reality that are simulated in simulation games are the things that will encourage us to adopt particular pre-existing constraints as we play. Simulations don't replicate reality, they gesture toward it. But they gesture toward it in specific ways that encourage us to engage with them as though they were real.

So, while the Game as Understood is contingent upon the Game as Experienced, and the Game as Experienced is contingent upon the Game as Designed, the contingencies flow the other way as well. No game is created in isolation—it is always created with a particular player and a particular context in mind. All game designs make assumptions (either implicit or explicit) about the pre-existing constraints that the player will bring to the experience. And all games provide cues (either intentionally or accidentally) to tell the player which of their pre-existing constraints apply.

INTERPRETIVE MOVES

When we make a move in a game, we change the game's state in some way. We pick up our queen and place her on a different square. We press the jump button and Mario jumps to a different platform. We flick the joystick and our car swerves to the left. That change in the game's state changes our active constraints, and that change of active constraints transports us to a new situation.

However, many of the constraints that structure any situation are internal. They're prior beliefs that we brought with us to the game, or they're internal analogs of the game's external constraints, or they're strategies that we've adopted in response to prior situations within the game. And because so many of the constraints that structure any situation are internal, it's possible for us to move from one situation to another without changing the external state of the game. Such a move is an *interpretive move*. When we make an interpretive move, we're not changing the state of the game, we're changing our attitude toward it.

What this means is that play is not limited to situations that offer choices between competing actions; it also occurs in situations that offer competing interpretations. "What should I do?" is a playful choice, but so are, "What's happening?" and, "What does this mean?" These interpretive choices may be directed toward the past ("What caused this?") or toward the future ("What's going to happen?"). They can even be directed toward ourselves ("Who am I?" or "Why am I doing this?"). If properly structured, these internal interpretive choices can be just as playful as choices that change the game's external state.

The most obvious examples of interpretive moves are the mental shifts we experience as we work through a puzzle. Sometimes, we try to solve puzzles by trial and error, putting the system in different states to see if any of them lead to a solution. But more often, we work though the puzzle in our heads, considering the implications of different approaches before we actually try any of them out. Sometimes, these mental shifts simply replicate and anticipate the normal moves we might make ("What happens if I put the red marble over here?"), but other times these mental shifts involve changes to our deeper understanding of the puzzle's structure ("What is that blue box for?").

An example of this sort of interpretive play can be found in *The Witness*. *The Witness* contains hundreds of puzzles, all of them variations on a simple theme—drawing a line from start to finish through some kind of maze. Sometimes, solving one of these puzzles is merely a matter of figuring out where the line should go. But more often, the challenge involves figuring out the maze's underlying grammar. "What do the black and white squares mean?" for example, or "Why are there dots at some of the intersections?" To solve the puzzle, you need to perform a sequence of interpretive moves until you arrive at a set of internal constraints that are functionally equivalent to the external constraints programmed into the game.

While this sort of interpretive play is easy to see in a puzzle game, it crops up in more action-oriented games as well. When you play a first-person shooter, many situations involve choosing between competing actions: Where should you aim? Where should you move? When should you reload? But some situations involve choosing between competing *interpretations*: Where did that enemy go? What does that explosion mean? What are my teammates doing?

These intervals of interpretive play can be just as satisfying as the action-oriented play that brackets them. It's fun to charge into a room full of enemies, blasting away. But it's also fun to creep stealthily along an empty corridor, trying to anticipate where your next threat will come from. In fact, entire games can be built around elaborated stretches of this kind of anticipatory play. Most horror games work this way—they deploy the occasional jump scare or violent attack to create a pervasive atmosphere of dread, and then let the player's imagination do the rest. The horror game experience relies less on the player actually encountering something scary and more on the player *thinking* about encountering something scary.

It's a short step from the interpretive play of a horror game like *Soma* to the interpretive play of an experiential game like *Dear Esther*. In *Dear Esther*, the player isn't trying to figure out where their next threat will come from. Rather, they're trying to figure out what's going on and what it all means. But the sorts of internal moves they make are similar. In both types of games the player works to discover a coherent set of internal constraints that are functionally equivalent to the game's external structure—they work to make sense of the game, to understand it in a way that explains and predicts the situations they encounter in the Game as Experienced.

SUMMARY

We experience play as a sequence of situations. These situations are structured by a changing system of active constraints. These active constraints determine what moves are available to us. When we make a move, we change our active constraints and transport ourselves to a new situation.

The constraints that structure the situations we encounter can be either external or internal. They can be imposed upon us by outside forces (like the laws of physics) or we can impose them upon ourselves (like our sense of strategy). But even when hard external constraints exist, they are often mirrored by softer internal analogs. We limit ourselves to the moves we believe are possible, regardless of what our external constraints actually allow.

Some moves change the external constraints the game imposes upon us, but other moves change the internal constraints we impose upon ourselves. These interpretive moves don't change the state of the game; they change our understanding of it. But, from our perspective as players, these internal moves can be just as playful and satisfying as moving a piece on the game board or pressing a button on the controller.

CHAPTER 3

Playfulness

A GOOD GAME IS PLAYFUL. It continually presents us with situations that are both challenging and engaging. It tightly holds our attention, without making us feel trapped by the hold that it has upon us. Instead, the experience is profoundly satisfying. We feel well-situated within the universe—both active and peaceful at the same time.

Playfulness is hard to evoke. Plenty of games don't manage it, and plenty of non-game experiences don't even attempt it. There is something special about how a good game is structured that causes playfulness to emerge. It's not merely a matter of imposing rules on the player—there are plenty of times when rules feel oppressive or frustrating. It's not merely a matter of putting the player in situations that offer choices—there are plenty of times when making choices feels stressful or confusing. Rather, playfulness is the result of having from the right sort of rules, arranged just so, rules that structure situations that engage and intrigue us.

Game design is the art of arranging rules just so. It's a tricky business, made more difficult by the fact that playfulness itself is dynamic. Playfulness is not a static property of a system of rules. Rather, it emerges from a system of rules as we play. Games do not *possess* playfulness; they *perform* it—over and over again, second by second, minute by minute, hour by hour, consistently.

If we want to design for playfulness, we need to understand how the static structure we create relates to the dynamic experience that the player encounters. The concepts that we developed in Chapter 2 allow us to do just that. Situations, constraints, and moves give us a way to understand how particular arrangements of rules intersect with our understanding to shape our moment-to-moment experience. They form a bridge between the Game as Designed, the Game as Experienced, and the Game as Understood.

Playful situations all share a universal structure. There is a particular way that the active constraints that shape a situation must be arranged in order for it to feel playful. This universal structure can be expressed by six broad heuristics:

- *Choice*: The right number of moves exists

- *Variety*: Situations don't repeat

- *Consequence*: Moves lead to new situations

- *Predictability*: New situations can be anticipated

- *Uncertainty*: New situations aren't predetermined

- *Satisfaction*: Desirable outcomes are attainable

These heuristics are the "rules for rules," as it were. They represent a hard-and-fast set of design principles that all games must obey. In the rest this chapter, we'll explore each of these heuristics in detail. We'll look at how playfulness emerges when these heuristics are followed, and how it falls apart when they are violated, and what design techniques we can to ensure the former is more common than the latter.

CHOICE

The most basic factor affecting the playfulness of a situation is the amount of choice it offers. Too little choice is bad, but so is too much. It's no fun to move a chess piece through a predetermined sequence of moves, but it's also no fun to aimlessly shift it from square to square without any restrictions at all. The rules of chess are tight enough to limit our moves to a handful of alternatives on each turn, but loose enough that there's almost always a choice to be made.

So, how many moves should a situation offer? Answering this question is difficult, because not all choices are equivalent. Three moves with wildly different outcomes can feel more playful than a dozen moves that all turn out pretty much the same. Also, it's not always easy to break down our opportunities for action into discretely countable moves. If we're playing an arcade racing game the analog steering wheel offers us a theoretically infinite number of possible actions, with each tiny increment of angle yielding a different trajectory down the track.

In practice however, a continuum of choices can usually be broken down into a handful of meaningful alternatives. In our hypothetical racing game there might be an infinite number of possible trajectories down the track, but many of them will produce more or less the same result. The actual moment-to-moment choices we face are more like, "Should I pass on the right or the left?" than, "Should I turn the steering wheel five degrees clockwise or six?"

How a player divides up a continuum of choices into a discrete set of moves depends upon their understanding of the situation. Multiple actions that lead to similar sets of new active constraints will be lumped together as one potential move. Even if there are an infinite number of subtly different things that can theoretically be done, in practice this multitude of possibilities usually collapses into a handful of meaningfully different alternatives.

Keeping all these caveats in mind, we can actually put hard bounds on the number of moves a situation should offer. Three to five moves per situation is best. One move is obviously not enough. If there's only one thing to do in a situation, then there is no choice at all, only the rote execution of a predetermined action. Two moves are better, but choosing between two alternatives is often trivial. For example, in the board game *Talisman* you can move either clockwise or counterclockwise after you roll the dice. But if the clockwise move lands you on a deadly dragon, you don't really have a choice—you move counterclockwise.

Three moves are where things start to get interesting. While there still might be a single best move out of the three, it takes more time to find it. This is because the *complexity* of comparing multiple alternatives increases geometrically. If there are only two moves there is only one comparison to make: "Is A better than B?" But if there are three moves then there are three comparisons: "Is A better than B? Is B better than C? Is C better than A?" Adding one more move triples the complexity of the situation. Determining the best of four moves requires six comparisons, determining the best of five moves requires ten comparisons, and so on (Figure 3.1).

The *immediate complexity* of a situation is the amount of work the player needs to do to pick the best move out of a collection of possible moves with obvious outcomes. It can be expressed by a simple formula:

$$Complexity = \frac{n * (n-1)}{2}$$

where n is the number of moves that the situation offers.

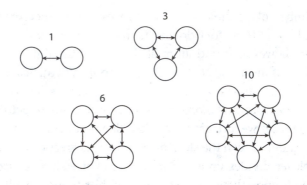

FIGURE 3.1   Geometric increase in complexity.

This is why situations quickly become overly complicated if they contain more than about five possible moves. Just adding one more move—going from five to six—increases the complexity from 10 to 15, a 50% increase. A situation with ten moves is *45 times* more complicated than a situation with two.

Choosing from among a large number of moves takes time, and so the pace of the game affects how many moves the player can handle. A slow, turn-based game like chess can support much greater complexity than a fast, real-time game like *Tetris*. Five moves is not an absolute upper bound—it can go higher if the player is given plenty of time to think about what they're going to do. Similarly, even choosing between two moves can be fun if the choice occurs under tight enough time constraints. Your only choice in an endless runner is, "Should I jump now?" but time pressure makes that simple choice feel playful. As a general rule, as the pace of a game increases, the number of choices the player faces should decrease.

Because so many different factors affect the number of moves a situation should have, it's often more useful to simply understand the effects of having either too many or too few. If we can recognize the symptoms of a situation that is over- or under-constrained, then we can fix it without having to figure out how many moves it should offer from first principles.

The range of choices we face in a situation is *the axis of play* (Figure 3.2). When we face a situation with too many possibilities for us to realistically consider, we feel *confused*. The potentialities of the moment overwhelm

FIGURE 3.2   Boredom vs. confusion.

us and we're not sure what we should do. We freeze. Or, we throw up our hands and make a move at random, unsure of whether it's a good move or not. In either case, our feeling of play collapses.

On the other hand, when we're faced with a situation with too few possibilities, we feel *bored*. Sometimes, this may be because there is no choice at all, or because the choice is a trivial one. But other times, it can be because the pace of the game is too slow. The choices we face may be individually interesting, but if they come too infrequently the game will still fail to engage us.

In general, it's better to err on the side of giving the player too many choices rather than too few. This is because the number of choices contained within a situation is partially determined by our own internal constraints. If a situation contains too many possibilities for us to consider, then we can always choose to ignore some of them to keep the game manageable. For example, when we first learn a fighting game, we might completely ignore the existence of the game's advanced combo moves; deciding which basic move to make is more than enough challenge.

Too few moves is a box that's much harder for us to escape. The only way to sustain play in an over-constrained game is to construct a separate meta-game that sits atop and feeds off the primary experience. This is the realm of griefing and trolling, as well as camp and satire. Even the dullest game can be made playful if the player creates their own play space, but it's generally better to try to anticipate the needs of the player, rather than forcing them to invent an idiosyncratic way to play.

VARIETY

The second heuristic is *variety*. The first time we encounter a situation it may feel playful, but if we encounter the same situation over and over again, it quickly becomes boring. That's because we remember the moves we made previously, and that knowledge becomes one of our internal constraints. Moves that turn out poorly are pruned from our choices, and moves that turn out well become more highly valued. Eventually, if we play through the same situation enough times, we no longer need to consider what the best move might be—we already know. And so, while theoretically the situation offers a choice, in practice it doesn't.

When we reach this point, the situation is *played out* or *exhausted*. Mechanically, there's still a choice to be made, but making it feels empty and pointless—we're just going through the motions. When a situation becomes played out we make our moves by rote, following an internal script laid down during our previous playthroughs. While we appear to be playing, the experience doesn't feel playful.

A good game doesn't just offer us situations that contain the right amount of choice. It also continually varies those situations, so each choice we face feels fresh. Before a situation becomes played out, it's replaced by a new situation that offers us a choice we haven't encountered before.

There are many ways to ensure that players always have fresh situations to play through. The simplest is the brute force approach: The designer handcrafts each one. This is how puzzles work. Puzzles present the player with a single unique situation (or at most a short chain of related situations) to play through. Once the player figures out the solution, the situation is exhausted. Working through a puzzle a second time isn't nearly as interesting, because our knowledge of the solution has become part of our internal constraints.

From a practical perspective, the problem with handcrafting situations is that it's extremely labor-intensive. It can take hours (or days) of brute force design work to create a set of constraints that a player might consume in only a few seconds. This is why most games use a combinatorial approach instead. The game (or game designer) rearranges a small number of elements or mechanics in different ways to create a large number of unique situations.

For example, chess only has six different types of pieces. However, these six types of pieces can be arranged in roughly 10^{50} different board positions. The variety we experience when we play chess emerges not because it has a large number of different mechanics, or because it has a large number of handcrafted situations, but because it has a small number of elements that can be arranged in a large number of unique ways—so many ways, in fact, that you can play chess your entire life and still continue to encounter unfamiliar situations. And even when you do encounter a situation more than once, you're unlikely to remember exactly what you did previously. There are just too many combinations for most players to hold in their heads.

A similar combinatorial approach is used in the design of first-person shooters. Situations within a first-person shooter are structured by a small number of elements: the geometry of the level, the positions and behaviors of the enemies, the player's own weaponry. However, because these elements can be deployed in different combinations, a huge number of situations can be created from a small number of assets. The same level can support a wide variety of unique encounters by changing the placement and number of enemies. Or the player can face the same enemies over and over again as long as the level layout is sufficiently different each time.

Game design is often less about designing situations themselves, and more about designing systems that will generate those situations. Sometimes, this means designing a set of rules (such as the rules of chess) that provide unique choices as the game's external state changes. Other times, this means designing a palette of game objects (like the enemies in a first-person shooter) that can be rearranged to create unique encounters. In both cases, however, the goal is to ensure that the player always experiences fresh situations without the designer having to handcraft every single moment of the game.

When designing a combinatorial system, there are several principles to keep in mind:

- *Make each element distinct*: Avoid creating two enemies that share the same behavior, or two mechanics that apply in similar situations. If different elements are too similar they won't increase variety.

- *Design for reuse*: Make sure different elements can actually be used in combination with each other. If a mechanic is only used once, consider cutting it, or expanding the game so that the mechanic is used more often.

- *Introduce elements gradually*: Add new mechanics only when you've nearly exhausted your previous mechanics. Too many elements introduced at the same time can be confusing.

Another source of variety are players themselves. Remember that each situation is structured not just by the game's rules, but by the player's own internal constraints. So as the player's understanding of the game changes, the situations they encounter will change as well, even if the external constraints imposed by the game remain the same.

For example, a novice player may ignore the combo moves in a fighting game because the basic move set provides enough variety to make the game interesting. But, as they play longer, those basic moves will gradually become exhausted. The existence of advanced combo moves gives expert players a set of mechanics that continue to generate interestingly unfamiliar situations long after the basic game is played out.

A game that offers long-term variety through under-constrained situations is called *deep*. Deep games present situations that contain advanced moves that novice players ignore. As novice players become more experienced, their early palette of basic moves becomes played out. But as these exhausted moves are pruned away, they're simultaneously replaced by intermediate and advanced moves that prevent the situation from becoming boring. In a deep game, a single set of external circumstances may present very different situations to players of different skill levels.

A major danger when designing depth is overwhelming the novice with too many choices. For this reason it's important that more advanced moves be masked from beginners so they don't at first appear to be viable choices. There are multiple ways to accomplish this:

- *Explicit difficulty levels*: The player chooses their skill level, and the game blocks certain actions for novice players. For example, a strategy game may not let the player perform trade or diplomacy if they're playing on easy mode.

- *Progression unlocks*: Certain moves may only become available after the player has passed milestones within the game that shows they have mastered the basics. In a role-playing game you might not unlock the grappling hook until you clear the swamp temple.

- *Execution difficulty*: Advanced moves may always be available, but be too technically difficult for a novice to execute. In a fighting game the more complicated combos may require a lot of practice to master, locking them away from beginners.

- *Hidden worth*: Advanced moves may always be accessible, but their strategic worth may be unclear. The best moves at the beginning of a real-time strategy game may seem pointless or worthless to the inexperienced player.

In practice, games often use a range of techniques to ensure that players always encounter fresh situations to play through. Handmade one-off situations are intermingled with combinatorially complex modular content. Core basic gameplay is expanded by the gradual inclusion of new mechanics. Advanced strategies are hidden away from the novice players, waiting to be discovered and exploited by the more experienced. And, finally, other players can provide a huge amount of variety. It takes much longer for a multiplayer game to become played out because our uncertainty over how the other player will respond makes even familiar situations feel fresh.

CONSEQUENCE

The third heuristic is *consequence*. In order for a game to feel playful, each move we make must transport us to a new situation. It's not enough for a game to just give us things to do. The things we do much change our circumstances in meaningful ways.

Opening a door, turning off a light, throwing a pebble—none of these actions are inherently playful. What makes them playful are the effect that have on the game world: Opening a drawer feels playful if we might discover a gold coin inside. Turning off a light feels playful if it makes it easier to hide from a monster. Throwing a pebble feels playful if we can use the sound to distract a sentry. It's not the action itself that matters, it's its *consequence*—the sense that we've changed our situation in a meaningful way.

An action without consequences is an *empty move*. Empty moves are moves that don't change our situation. Performing them leaves the same active constraints in force, and so they feel pointless. A choice that doesn't affect our active constraints isn't a choice. Furthermore, a move only feels consequential if we realize that it changed something. A move with hidden consequences is indistinguishable from a move with none. It's not enough for consequences to exist merely in the Game as Designed. They must also exist in the Game as Understood.

Sometimes, the consequences of a move are immediate and obvious. If we're playing a platformer and we jump from one platform to another, it's clear that our situation has changed. But with other games, the effects of our actions can be less clear. If we're playing a first-person shooter and we shoot at an enemy, it might be hard for us to tell if our bullets hit their target. So most shooters provide explicit *cues* to confirm that the enemy was hit—a splash of blood, an impact sound, a special animation. These cues aren't merely gratuitous gore. They make our moves feel consequential. They inform us that our actions have transported us to a new situation.

Cuing consequence is particularly important when the effects of a move play out over a long time. In *SimCity*, building a police station has many consequences. It lowers the crime rate, increases property values, and boosts tax revenues. However, none of those effects are obvious when the station is built. They all lie minutes or hours in the future. In order for building the station to feel playful, its construction needs to be accompanied by short-term cues that hint at these long-term effects—a graph that shows the plunging crime rate, a visual overlay that shows the rising property values. This information is not merely a convenience; it's essential to the playfulness of the experience.

When designing cues, it's important to keep in mind that they are not simply a way to transmit raw information. Each cue is a tool for shaping the player's internal constraints. How a cue is presented to the player determines the new situation they will occupy in the Game as Understood.

With this in mind, there are a number of principles to consider when designing cues:

- *Cues should follow immediately after moves*: The purpose of a cue is to make the move feel consequential. The longer the delay, the weaker its connection to the move, and the less effective it will be.

- *Cues should direct attention to the consequence, not the move itself*: If you swing your sword and hit the dragon, the dragon should flash red, not the sword. If you pull a lever to open a distant gate, you should hear the sound of the gate opening, not the lever being pulled.

- *The size of the cue implies the size of the consequence*: Small, bland cues imply that the move didn't do very much, while large, vivid cues imply the consequences of the move were huge.

- *Similar cues imply similar consequences*: If different moves have similar consequences they should be similarly cued. If a splash of blood conveys damage during a fight, a similar splash of blood should also be used to convey falling damage. If cues are different, players will assume the difference is significant.

- *Failure should be cued*: Missed shots, locked doors, failed attacks—all of these circumstances should have small cues to tell the player the move didn't work.

- *Empty moves should not be cued*: If a move doesn't do anything, don't mislead the player into thinking that it might. Temporarily locked doors should rattle when you try to open them. Windows that can never be opened should remain silent.

- *Too many overlapping cues are confusing*: Cues are only effective if they can be deciphered. If everything the player does is accompanied by a large and distinctive cue, then the game will degenerate into a cacophony of uninterpretable noise.

- *Un-cued consequences sometimes have uses*: Un-cued consequences can be used to hide the worth of advanced moves in deep games.

When designing a cue, the primary question should always be: How does this cue change the player's active constraints? The purpose of a cue is to shift the player to a new situation within the Game as Understood. The particular information that's presented in the cue determines what this new situation will be.

Because consequences exist primarily in our minds, it's even possible for us to make consequential moves without changing the game's external state. If you're crouched in a dungeon corridor, wondering if there might be a dragon lurking around the next corner, the outcome of that speculation is a consequence. Believing that there a dragon waiting for you changes your situation. You'll make different moves than if you believe the way ahead is clear. This is how purely interpretive play can be consequential even though it doesn't change the external state of the game. Trying to figure out what something means, imagining how something might play out—these ways of playing don't have external consequences in the game world, but they do have internal consequences within the Game as Understood.

In fact, the notion of consequence is particularly useful when designing interpretive play because it helps us distinguish between actual interpretive moves from *empty speculation*. Interpretive play is not just "thinking about the game." It's thinking about the game in a way that affects our future thoughts or actions. It's thinking about the game in a way that has consequences.

So speculating about whether there's a dragon around the corner feels playful because the conclusion we arrive at matters. It changes our active constraints. Similarly, wondering if our best general is a traitor feels playful because the consequences of deciding one way or another are significant. It will change how we act toward her, the missions we send her on, the troops we assign to her. Our speculation feels meaningful.

We can contrast these examples of meaningful interpretive play with other ways of thinking about a game that don't have the same sort of play value. For example, instead of wondering if there's a dragon around the corner, we might wonder if the walls have moss growing on them. The problem with this sort of empty speculation is that it doesn't lead anywhere. Whichever way we decide, our overall situation remains the same.

The presence or absence of moss won't change our active constraints within the Game as Understood.

Empty speculation is the internal analog of the empty move. It resembles an interpretive move in that we're making a decision regarding our understanding of the game. But it doesn't feel playful because it doesn't change our opportunities for making future decisions. In order to feel playful, an interpretive move must change our internal attitudes in a way that matters.

PREDICTABILITY

The fourth heuristic is *predictability*. In order for a situation to feel playful, it's not enough for moves to have consequences. Players also need to have a general idea of what those consequences will be in advance.

The importance of predictability is tied to the existence of goals. When we play a game we don't make moves haphazardly. We make them with some purpose in mind. With many games that purpose is to win; the game's rules lay out an arbitrary win condition—some situation we're trying to work toward—and we assess the worth of our moves according to whether they carry us toward that situation or away from it. Good moves help us win, and bad moves make us lose.

But we can only assess the worth of a move if we can predict what its outcome will be. If we move the joystick to the right, it's not enough for the character to do any random thing. Our character needs to do an expected thing. (Most likely, move to the right.) If moving the joystick to the right sometimes moves us right, and sometimes moves us left, and sometimes makes us jump, then choosing feels pointless, even though it's consequential. We're no longer choosing between different alternatives; we're simply triggering a random event.

Games are playful because they are predictable. They're structured so that there's a clear connection between cause and effect. That clear connection makes our moves feel meaningful and our choices feel significant. Our moves change our situation in predictable ways, and, because our moves change our situation in predictable ways, we are able to weigh the worth of different moves based on how they help us accomplish our goals.

Furthermore, this predictability allows us to string together a sequence of potential moves into a causal chain. Each move is no longer considered as an isolated event, but rather as the first step in a cascade of moves that stretches seconds, minutes, or even hours into the future. So we move our character to the right not because moving our character to the right immediately wins the game. We move to the right because moving to the right lets us peek around the pillar, and peeking around the pillar lets us shoot an arrow at the dragon, and shooting an arrow at the dragon helps us win the game. The value of most moves is determined not in isolation, but by the potential future situations that choosing it makes possible.

How do we ensure that our moves have predictable consequences? There are four main techniques for cuing causality:

- *Familiarity*: From our experiences in the real world (and other games) we know that certain actions are likely to have certain consequences. If you shoot someone with a gun, they get hurt. If you crash a car into a wall, it doesn't run as well. When we're assessing the worth of different moves, we begin with the assumption that their consequences will mirror our existing understanding.

- *Proximity*: When things happen in close proximity to each other, either in time or in space, we assume that they're causally related. If a row of *Tetris* blocks vanishes the moment the last gap in the row is filled, then we assume that filling the last gap caused the row to vanish. When we encounter unfamiliar causal relations in a game, we connect cause and effect by noticing that they coincide in time, or space, or both.

- *Continuity*: Once a causal relationship is established, it persists. If we press a button to throw a grenade, then an initial causal relationship between the button press and the grenade is established by its proximate appearance. But the persistence of the grenade in the world maintains the causal link. When the grenade explodes five seconds later, we connect the explosion back to our initial button press, and not to other events that might have occurred in closer proximity.

- *Repetition*: Even in the absence of familiarity, proximity, and continuity we can still discover causal relationships if they're repeated often enough. For example, suppose a lever in a castle opens and closes a distant gate. Without proximity and continuity to help us link cause and effect, it can take us a long time to correlate the position of the lever with the state of the gate. But, if we spend enough time exploring the castle and playing with the lever we'll eventually discover the connection.

Games make use of all of these techniques. Most moves do exactly what we expect them to do. Deviations from the familiar are cued by immediate feedback. Longer-term effects are linked back to their causes through continuity—objects persist in the game world to remind us of the events we've set in motion. And causal links are repetitive—similar causes produce similar effects, allowing us to eventually notice the connection even in the absence of other cues.

The clear cuing of causality gives games a clarity that the real world lacks. In the real world, we're often unsure of the ramifications of our actions. Our way forward is often murky, and we frequently experience unintended consequences or random setbacks. Part of what makes games feel playful is the predictability of their systems. When we choose to do something in a game, we know what the outcome is likely to be. We can work purposely toward a goal, secure in the knowledge that our work won't be undone by unfairness or inconsistency.

Predictability is also important for interpretive moves. It's not enough for our speculations to have consequences—we also need to have some sense of what those consequences might be. So, wondering if there's a dragon waiting around the corner only feels playful if we have some sense of what encountering a dragon might involve. If we have no idea what to expect from a dragon, then making a decision about its presence or absence won't change our internal situation. The fact the encounter itself might later turn out to be consequential is not enough. It's our advance knowledge of those consequences and how they relate to our goals that makes the speculation feel playful.

UNCERTAINTY

Given the importance of predictability as a design heuristic, it would be easy to assume that the more predictable a game, the better. If players need to be able to direct themselves toward a specific goal as they play, it might seem as though it would be best to make sure that the outcome of every move is completely obvious and unambiguous.

But if we look at actual games, we discover that this is rarely the case. Virtually all games include specific mechanisms to introduce uncertainty into the outcomes of our moves. In *Monopoly*, we roll dice to determine how far we can move. In *Super Mario Bros.*, we execute jumps under time pressure, increasing our chances of making a mistake. In baseball, the trajectory of a line drive is the product of a complicated and unpredictable physical interaction between ball and bat. Even in a game like chess where the immediate outcome of a move is unambiguous, the unforeseen countermoves of our opponent cast a veil over the more distant future.

Why should this be? If playfulness is a function of our capacity to choose our course through the game, why should we enjoy experiences that contain so much potential for our intentions to be thwarted?

To answer these questions we need to revisit the notion of the exhausted situation. In the section on variety, we looked at how our sense of choosing can be eroded by our memories of our past choices. If we repeatedly encounter the same situation, we remember what our previous moves were and those memories constrain our current circumstances. If we play through the same situation over and over, our sense of making a choice evaporates and the situation becomes played out.

Something similar happens if we can perfectly predict the outcome of our moves. If we know exactly what our situation will be after we make a move, then we can anticipate what our next move will be, and the move after that, and the move after that. We can plan a whole series of moves in advance, our future situations stretching out ahead of us in a long chain of cause and effect. As a result, when it comes time to actually make one of the moves we've planned, it no longer feels like a choice. We already used up the choice when we first thought our way through the chain.

So, while we need to be able to roughly predict the effect of our actions, our predictions should always be imperfect. Each time we make a move we should never be quite sure that it will unfold exactly the way we expect. The uncertainty prevents future situations from becoming exhausted before we reach them. Even if our plans come to fruition and events turn out how we expected, we should still have doubts about whether our previous plans are still valid. We should feel compelled to revisit our previous assessment of our circumstances, reconsidering whether our anticipated moves really are the best choice after all.

Uncertainty is the fifth heuristic. And there are a variety of ways to achieve it:

- *Random chance*: Many games use explicit random-number generators to hide the future from us. If a future situation is determined by the roll of a die, we can't play through it in advance.

- *Hidden information*: We also can't play through a future situation if we don't know all the constraints that structure it. In many card games, we know which cards we hold, but not which cards are held by the other players. This lack of information prevents us from perfectly anticipating how the game will unfold.

- *Intractable complexity*: Even if information isn't hidden, there can be too much of it for us to process in a short amount of time. Fast-paced games sometimes hide the future in plain sight; we have perfect information about future situations, but no time to analyze it.

- *Real-world physics*: This is a common technique used by many sports to introduce uncertainty. The exact way that a ball will bounce is hard to predict. The variation introduced by the physical behavior of the system prevents perfect knowledge of future situations.

- *Human motor skills*: This technique is closely related to the previous one. Moves in sports tend to be very sensitive to initial conditions; slight variations in how we swing a baseball bat or a tennis racket can lead to large variations in the outcome. Action video games use similar techniques, where the outcome of a move is determined by the exact timing of a button press.

- *Other players*: Even when we know exactly how a game system will behave, the presence of other players (either competitively or cooperatively) introduces uncertainty. We can never be quite sure what they'll do.

It's important to keep in mind that randomness and uncertainty are not inherently playful. A game isn't made better by introducing uncertainty for its own sake, and too much uncertainty violates the previous heuristic. Uncertainty should only be deployed to prevent future situations from being preemptively exhausted. It should always be used to make sure that each choice is experienced when it's actually encountered.

Uncertainty is also important in interpretive play. We should never be quite sure that our interpretations are absolutely correct. We should always feel as though our judgments are provisional—they're always open to revision. If we *know* conclusively that there's a dragon around the corner, there's no further reason to engage in interpretive play. The situation has been resolved and we move on to planning what we do next. But if we only *suspect* there might be a dragon, then interpretive play is sustained. We keep coming back to our decision, revisiting it, and reconsidering our conclusions.

Designing an interesting interpretive situation is not merely a matter of posing an interesting question to the player. The question also should also lack an easy, obvious answer. Resolving an interpretive question should always leave the player with a lingering doubt about either their answer's correctness or its ramifications. It should invite the player to revisit the question over and over, reconsidering the implications of their choices. This epistemic uncertainty prevents the player from quickly racing through a long chain of trivial interpretations, quickly resolving them and preempting future play.

SATISFACTION

Sometimes, a game is too hard. We have a goal that we're trying to accomplish, but no matter what we do, the game defeats us. Maybe our reactions are too slow. Maybe we don't have enough endurance. Maybe our grasp of strategy is too weak. Maybe we misunderstand what the point of the game really is. Regardless of the reason, we repeatedly find ourselves in situations where every move leads to a bad outcome.

As players, we can tolerate temporary setbacks. But if all we experience is repeated failure, then our tolerance will fray. Even if we encounter a wide variety of new situations and our moves within those situations have predictable consequences—even if all the other heuristics are obeyed—we will nevertheless feel frustrated and dissatisfied.

The final heuristic is *satisfaction*. In order for a situation to feel playful, we need to feel as though it offers us the possibility of success. There needs to be at least one move that leads to a positive outcome, and that move needs to be accessible to us given our current knowledge and skill.

At the same time, however, there need to be other moves that are less desirable. There needs to be the possibility of failure. We need to be able to win, but we also need to be able to lose, and we need to be able to tell the difference between the winning and losing moves before we make them.

The reason for this is related to our need to feel as though our choices matter. The third heuristic says that different moves need to have different consequences—they need to lead to different situations. However, it's not enough for these different situations to merely have different active constraints. They also need to have different *worth*. Choosing between two different situations doesn't feel like a meaningful choice if they both are equally valuable. So, playful situations need to offer a collection of moves with a range of worth. There need to be both good moves and bad moves.

If all our moves are good, or all our moves are bad, our choice no longer feels like it matters and play collapses.

The worth of a move is determined by considering it in relation to the game's goals. Does this move carry me closer to some preferred situation or further away? In a game of basketball, the goal is to score more baskets than the opposing team. So any move that leads to scoring a basket (or prevents your opponent from scoring) is a good move. And any move that leads to your opponent scoring a basket (or prevents your team from scoring) is a bad move.

While playful situations need to have both good and bad moves, they are made more interesting if the determination of relative goodness or badness is nontrivial. A situation with one good move is not as playful as a situation with a range of moves of uncertain value. If one move is obviously superior, then deciding to perform it isn't much of a decision. Deciding which of two platforms to jump to is interesting; deciding whether to jump to a platform or into a pit of spikes isn't.

There are several ways to create interesting tension between the worth of different moves:

- *Conflicting goals*: If we have several different criteria for assessing the worth of a move, then the task of picking the best move becomes much more interesting. If we're trying to both capture the enemy base and stay alive, we will often encounter situations in which a good move for accomplishing one goal is a bad move for accomplishing the other.

- *Different time frames*: Even if we only have a single goal that we're working toward, tension can still exist between different moves if their rewards pay out over different time frames. Which is better, a small short-term reward, or a large long-term one?

- *Different probabilities*: Choosing between a small reward that's certain and a large reward that's risky generates the same sort of tension. There's not one move that's obviously superior, and so the decision we make feels significant and meaningful.

If every move is a good move, then our sense that we're making a choice collapses. All moves become equivalent to each other and the game becomes boring. We feel like we're just going through the motions as we continue to play. On the other hand, if every move is a bad move then our

FIGURE 3.3   Frustration, boredom, and confusion.

boredom turns into *frustration*. Rather than there being a single obvious and dull way to move forward, it seems like there's no way to move forward at all.

The addition of frustration gives us a fuller perspective of the axis of play (Figure 3.3). Play is highly sensitive to the number of choices we face from moment to moment. Too many and the situation is confusing. Too few and the situation is boring. None at all and the situation flips from boredom to frustration. Any of these can cause playfulness to collapse.

Satisfaction also affects interpretive play. When we're in an interpretive situation, we need to feel like there's an answer to the question we're considering. If we can't make any sense of the circumstances we find ourselves in, we will feel frustrated in just the same way that we feel frustrated when all of our moves are bad ones.

SUMMARY

A game is an engine for repeatedly generating playful situations. A situation feels playful when its constraints are arranged such that it holds our attention without making us feel confined or trapped. It offers us freedom of movement, but limits us to a handful of distinct moves.

We can gauge the playfulness of a situation by plotting its position on the axis of play. A situation with too many moves is confusing. One with too few is boring. A situation with no moves at all is frustrating. There are six heuristics we can use to help us understand where a situation falls on the axis of play: choice, variety, consequence, predictability, uncertainty, and satisfaction.

Playful situations offer us a handful of moves to choose from, with the number increasing in inverse relation to the pace of the game. If the same situation repeats over and over, it ceases to be playful because we remember which moves we made previously. Similarly, if the outcome of a situation is too predictable, we'll play through future situations in our heads, exhausting them preemptively before we reach them. If two moves produce the same outcome, choosing between them won't feel like a choice—different moves should have different consequences. These consequences need to be predictable enough that we can weigh the worth of our moves in relation our goals, but not so predictable that our future moves are preemptively exhausted. And finally, there should always be at least one move that feels like it offers a way forward. If our goals seem completely unattainable, the game feels pointless.

CHAPTER 4

Anticipation

I N C HAPTER 3, WE looked at what factors make individual situations feel playful. However, our analysis focused primarily on *immediate play*. In immediate play, the situations we encounter are linked together in a linear chain and each move carries us forward to the next situation.

This model works well enough for fast-paced action games that demand quick decisions—shooters, racing games, endless runners. From moment to moment we try to choose the move that does the best job of steering the flow of the game toward our goal. The constant stream of new situations means that there are always meaningful choices for us to make.

However, this model has a harder time accounting for the experience of playing a slower strategic game. When we play this sort of game, our interactions don't come in a rapid, continuous stream. They may occur seconds or even minutes apart. But even though our interactions might be intermittent, our feeling of play is continuous. We're still playing even though we're not constantly interacting.

In order to understand this sort of game, we need to introduce the concept of *anticipatory play*. When we're engaged in anticipatory play we're not moving linearly through a chain of situations. Rather, we're exploring a tree of possibilities. Anticipatory play involves navigating the ramifications of this tree, racing through branching hypothetical situations to discover where they lead, and then backtracking to investigate other possibilities.

While the situations we encounter during anticipatory play aren't arranged in a linear chain, they still obey the heuristics: Each situation in the tree should offer a handful of moves. Situations shouldn't repeat, and different moves should have different outcomes. In order to move through the tree at all, we need to be able to predict what the outcome of a move will be. But in order for our explorations not to be trivial, we should be uncertain that our predictions are accurate. And, finally, our anticipation should allow for a positive resolution—we need to be able to distinguish good situations from bad, and find a move that leads to a good one.

Racing forward and back through a tree of possibilities is what gives strategic games their particular texture. From moment to moment we're not deciding what to do. Rather, we're discovering what's *possible* to do. It's the exploration of the tree that holds our attention. Our actual interactions with the game, when they occur, are often a matter of bookkeeping. The fun in chess doesn't come from moving a pawn—it comes from considering all the ways a pawn can move.

While we primarily encounter anticipatory play in slower strategic games, we can also experience flashes of it in fast-paced action games. When we're playing a first-person shooter, most of our attention will be occupied by the immediate challenges of dodging and aiming, but mixed in with these immediate moves will be brief bursts of anticipatory play. During these moments we don't interact with the game. Rather, we explore the possibility of space structured by our current constraints, trying to figure out where our next enemy will come from, or what our best escape route is.

CHARACTERISTICS OF ANTICIPATORY PLAY

In Chapter 3, we introduced the idea of immediate complexity. Immediate complexity is the amount of work required to identify the best move in a situation. It scales quadratically as the number of moves increases. This quadratic increase is the reason that situations with more than a handful of moves quickly become confusing.

Anticipatory complexity is a related concept. Anticipatory complexity takes into account that the worth of a move can't always be determined by looking at the move's immediate consequences. Sometimes, you have to consider long chains of hypothetical consequences to determine the best move. So, the anticipatory complexity of a situation is not just a function of the number of moves the situation offers. It's also a function of the average number of situations you need to look ahead. Here's the formula:

$$Anticipatory\ Complexity = \frac{m^n * (m^n - 1)}{2}$$

where m is the average number of situations you need to look ahead, and n is the average number of moves per situation.

While immediate complexity scales quadratically, anticipatory complexity scales exponentially—a much more rapid increase. Looking more than a couple of moves ahead can generate a huge number of possibilities. If each situation has three viable moves and you anticipate three moves in the future, you have 351 comparisons to make to determine which sequence of moves is the best. If each situation has five viable moves and you anticipate five moves in the future, then the number of comparisons is almost five million.

If we're considering how a complicated chain of moves might unfold, we don't actually perform five million brute force comparisons. Instead, we use our strategic knowledge to prune the tree of possibilities, discarding some moves out of hand without considering their ramifications. This approach means that sometimes we might miss good moves whose worth isn't immediately obvious, but it does keep the problem tractable.

Anticipatory complexity limits the number of moves we can analyze during anticipatory play. The farther into the future we need to look to determine the worth of a move, the fewer moves each situation can have. Even if each situation only offers two or three moves, a game can still feel overwhelmingly complex if determining the best move requires us to look a dozen moves ahead. The exponential growth of anticipatory complexity leaves us feeling confused by our options, and play collapses.

Anticipatory complexity is affected by uncertainty. If the outcome of a move is uncertain, then we need to accommodate all possible outcomes within our situation tree. Adding a little randomness makes it much harder to determine the best move in a situation, because randomness multiplies the number of branches in the tree and increases the anticipatory complexity. In general, the more important anticipatory play is to a game, the less random it should be.

Anticipatory play takes time. While it's true that we can imagine the unfolding of a chain of situations far more quickly than we can actually play through them, the speed of our imagination is not infinite. If we play a game that involves a great deal of anticipation, we may spend minutes or even hours considering the consequences before we make a move.

The time we spend in anticipatory play requires stillness. In order for this kind of play to occur, the game needs to make room for it. If we're always immersed in the demands of immediate play, then we won't have time to plan or analyze. This is why sometimes the most playful thing a game can do is hold still. Non-interactive play emerges in the moments when the immediate demands of a game are kept at bay so that the player can plan or consider.

Just as with immediate play, an anticipatory play space can become exhausted. Once we've thoroughly explored the tree, there's no play in continuing to analyze the same situations over and over again. We see this effect if one player takes too long to take their turn during a board game. Off-turn play is anticipatory—when it's not our turn, we spend our time analyzing our circumstances and planning what to do next. This off-turn play can be fun and engaging, but if it goes on too long, we run out of hypotheticals to explore. We're bored until our turn comes around again. The design of such a game requires matching the duration of its periods of stillness to the anticipatory complexity of its situation tree. Games with large, ramified situation trees can support longer periods of stillness than games with small, simple ones.

Another factor in the design of anticipatory games is *context switching*. Context switching arises because the active constraints that structure anticipatory play are often different from the active constraints that structure immediate play, and there's a cognitive cost associated with swapping between these different sets of active internal constraints.

What this means is that when we finish a rapid run of immediate challenges it often takes a few moments for us to stop thinking about our next move and drop into anticipatory play. And similarly if we're deep in anticipatory play, it's hard to suddenly switch gears and respond to an immediate challenge. The beginning and ending of an interval of anticipatory play both need to be shaped to accommodate this context switch.

Transitions from immediate to anticipatory play should be cued with a *threshold*. A threshold is a clear boundary that tells player there's been a significant change in context; it's a shift in the overall texture of the experience. It can be as simple as passing through a door or turning a corner, but it can also be represented by a change in lighting, or effects, or visual style. It can be abstract as well as physical. Pausing time is a threshold, as is the "letterbox" effect that indicates a cut scene. A threshold is anything that signals to the player that their circumstances have significantly changed and they should pause to reconsider their active constraints.

Not only should games provide thresholds at moments when there's an intended transition from immediate to anticipatory play, they should also avoid them when no such transition is intended. Continuous action sequences shouldn't flow across dramatic visual boundaries, for example,

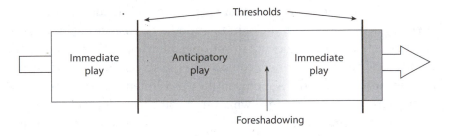

FIGURE 4.1   Cuing transitions between immediate and anticipatory play.

because any major change in circumstances can flip the player from immediate to anticipatory play. Abrupt changes in context will produce hitches in the immediate play experience as players fruitlessly try to orient themselves within their new circumstances.

Transitions from anticipatory play back to immediate play should be cued with *foreshadowing*. While a threshold is an abrupt boundary, foreshadowing is more gradual. It's a warning to the player that they need to temporarily suspend their exploration of the situation tree and focus their attention on the moment-to-moment play. A glimpse of a monster lurking ahead, the sound of a sentry chambering a round, the fade-to-black at the end of a cut scene—these sorts of cues foreshadow a return to immediate play. The player shouldn't be dropped unexpectedly into an immediate challenge, but rather be given a foreshadowing cue so they have a few moments to prepare themselves before the action resumes.

In general, transitions from immediate to anticipatory play are cued abruptly and transitions from anticipatory to immediate play are cued gradually (Figure 4.1). In both cases, the goal is to help the player switch smoothly from one set of active constraints to another.

CUING CLOSURE

While foreshadowing can be used to warn the player to temporarily suspend anticipatory play, sometimes we want to shut it down altogether. For example, if the player has been using brief intervals of stillness to plot how to rescue the princess, we need to guide them to wrap up their plotting shortly before the rescue actually unfolds.

This is *closure*. Closure is the sense that we're finished with a particular anticipatory play space. Whatever question we were asking ourselves has been answered. And furthermore, the answer is neither temporary nor provisional. It's final and conclusive so we don't feel any desire to go back and reassess our anticipatory moves.

The easiest way to understand how closure works is to look at situations where it's denied. Suppose you're in the middle of an exciting boss battle and the electrical power goes out in your neighborhood. Your mind is still racing ahead to plan your next combo, but the screen is dark and there's nothing more you can do. A moment like this is intensely frustrating. The situation tree comes crashing down around you as the play space abruptly collapses. The game is over, but you have no closure because your anticipatory play didn't wind down cleanly.

The denial of closure occurs whenever the end of anticipatory play doesn't line up with the end of the experience. Our external circumstances may dictate that the game is over, but our minds are still sifting through contingencies that can never be resolved. Technically the game is done, but it doesn't *feel* done.

This frustration can occur even when the end of the game isn't caused by something as drastic as a power failure. Winning a game through an unexpected fluke can trigger a similar response. There's hollowness to this sort of win. Rather than the rush of triumph that victory usually brings, we find ourselves feeling stunned and disappointed. We won, but we weren't ready to win, and so the satisfaction of winning is denied us.

Closure is achieved by gradually shutting down the player's avenues for anticipatory play as the end approaches. One reason that boss battles are effective conclusions is that they discourage players from thinking any further into the future: Don't worry about conserving ammo, or whether you're on the right path, or what's going to happen next—just focus all your effort and attention on defeating this giant squid *right now*.

There are a number of techniques that can be used to trigger closure:

- *Immediate challenges*: As mentioned previously, if the demands of immediate play are particularly intense they can crowd out our opportunities for anticipatory play. The longer the immediate challenge persists, the more difficult it is for us to return to the constraints that governed our previous anticipatory play. Long boss battles or other intense action sequences can "wipe the slate clean" and move us toward closure.

- *Progress cues*: These often take the form of explicit meters or counters, but they can also be more subtle, like a map that shows which areas you've visited and which you haven't. If you're on a quest to kill 20 goblins, it's very satisfying to have a counter that tracks your kills, even though it doesn't have any effect on your immediate tactics. The counter isn't there to help you kill goblins—it's there to help you stop thinking about killing goblins when the quest is over.

- *Strategic resolves*: If a game offers a variety of long-term goals, these goals should gradually be accomplished as the end of the game draws near. At the same time, no new goals should be added. Side quests should be introduced near the beginning of a game, not near the end. As the end of the game approaches, the player's attention should be focused on the conclusion, not on any extraneous unfinished business.

- *Advancement plateaus*: Another way to signal that the end is approaching is to slow the player's progress to a crawl. There may still be things for the player to do, but they accomplish less and less. It takes longer and longer for the player's character to level up. Crafting and skill trees have fewer slots to unlock. Anticipatory planning feels pointless, because there's no longer anything meaningful to do.

- *Linear situations*: And finally, a good indication that anticipatory play is winding down is that the game starts limiting our moves. The path ahead becomes more linear and obvious. This linearity would feel boring if we encountered it earlier in the game; when it comes at the end of the game, it does an excellent job of triggering closure. If we can clearly perceive the shape of the ending ahead of us, there's no longer any reason to keep exploring our situation tree.

Immediate play doesn't need closure because it's always focused on our moment-to-moment circumstances. It naturally winds down when we reach a game state where there are no longer any useful moves to make. But anticipatory play takes place within a framework of internal constraints and is directed toward the future events. The inwardly directed nature of anticipatory play means that even if there's nothing left to do in the external game, we still may be playing an anticipatory game in our own minds. Players need to be guided toward a graceful resolution of this internal play space.

THE RESULT OF ANTICIPATORY PLAY

The result of anticipatory play is not a change in the game's external state, but a shift in our internal constraints. This shift can manifest itself in several ways:

- *A plan*: A plan is a sequence of moves that we've worked out in advance. Our internal constraints shift so that when we arrive at each expected situation during immediate play, we give priority to the moves that follow the plan. "I should toss a hand grenade through the open window and then rush in!" is a plan.

- *A prediction*: A prediction is an expectation of how the game will unfold regardless of which moves we make. Our internal constraints define a hypothetical future that we can use to filter our immediate moves. "There are monsters waiting for me around the next corner!" is a prediction.

- *A strategy*: A strategy is a generalized plan. It's the discovery of some broad rule that helps us determine the best move across multiple situations. It's a new set of constraints that apply not just to our current circumstances, but to the game at large. "Our team should work together as a group!" is a strategy.

- *An interpretation*: An interpretation is a generalized prediction. It's a broad way of thinking about the game that explains why it's unfolding the way it is. It's not just figuring out what's likely to happen next, but figuring out why things are happening. "One of my allies is a traitor!" is an interpretation.

In each of these cases, our anticipatory play leads us to adopt new internal constraints that prune away undesirable branches of the situation tree, stripping it down to a linear chain of expectations. These expectations represent what we think will happen (a prediction), or what we think we should do (a plan), and they are structured by new strategies and interpretations.

The role of changing strategies and interpretations in anticipatory play is particularly significant. Because anticipatory moves can trigger shifts in the internal constraints that define the situation tree, the tree itself is in flux as we play. This is why we can revisit the same node multiple times during anticipatory play without violating the variety heuristic. The tree itself is continually shifting along with our internal constraints, so we can revisit an old node without it feeling played out.

When we engage in anticipatory play we're not merely trying to discover a desirable path through a static tree of situations. We're trying to discover a set of constraints that defines a tree that permits the existence of a desirable path. Anticipatory play is not merely exploratory, it's also constructive, and it is the constructive aspect of the experience that gives it much of its depth and power.

CRUXES

Whether it's a plan or a prediction, the outcome of interpretive play always contains within it an implicit expectation of the future. Whether it's through our own agency, or merely through the natural unfolding of the game around us, our new internal constraints are an encapsulation of how we believe the game will go. We expect to encounter certain situations, and we intend to act in certain ways when those situations arise.

But sometimes our expectations are wrong. The moves we make lead to failure instead of success. The unforeseen happens, and we find ourselves in circumstances we never anticipated: We understeer and crash our car into a wall. We're surrounded by goblins. Our opponent captures our queen. We miss a jump and fall to our doom. We've failed.

Such a moment is a *crux*. A crux is a rupture between the Game as Experienced and the Game as Understood. It's an indication that our predictive capacities have gone awry, and that our previous anticipatory play has led us down the wrong path. Our conception has diverged from reality.

When a crux occurs, we experience it as a moment of frustration. This frustration is similar to the frustration we feel when a situation doesn't seem to offer us any way forward. We've been thwarted from achieving our goals, and we find ourselves in an undesirable situation.

However, unlike the extended frustration of not being able to see any way forward, the frustration of a crux is fleeting. Instead of triggering a collapse of the play space, this fleeting frustration initiates a fresh cascade of anticipatory play. During this new round of anticipatory play, our prior failure works as a constraint on the situation tree. We avoid making moves that we now know are likely to fail, and we avoid making predictions that we now know are likely to be incorrect.

So while a crux is a moment of frustration, it also is a moment of opportunity. Because it represents a rupture between external reality and internal conception, a crux is a chance to *learn*, to bring our internal conceptions more closely in line with the external reality that they are directed toward. In fact, this is how we learn through play—not by the game telling us things, but by the game putting us in situations where our expectations are thwarted, causing us to engage in anticipatory play to resolve the challenge of the crux.

The notion of the crux allows for a more general understanding of the relationship between immediate and anticipatory play, and between satisfaction and frustration. When we're immersed in immediate play, our play space is structured by our own internal constraints—our understanding of the game and the strategies that will allow us to succeed within it. As we move from situation to situation within immediate play we choose our moves according to these internal constraints. We have a sense of what the best move is from moment to moment, and choosing this move and having it succeed is profoundly satisfying.

However, sometimes we choose the wrong move. Or even if we don't explicitly choose the wrong move, the game unfolds in a way that we didn't anticipate. This triggers a crux—a fleeting moment of frustration caused by the realization that our conception of the game doesn't align with its reality. The crux kicks off a cascade of anticipatory play—a reassessment of our understanding of the game and our plans for future moves. The outcome of this anticipatory play is a shift in our internal constraints—a new understanding or strategy that (hopefully) is more in line with the Game as Experienced. And then, armed with these new internal constraints, we reenter the cycle of immediate play (Figure 4.2).

The new internal constraints that emerge from the resolution of a crux are not necessarily optimal. When a game unfolds in a way we don't expect, we explore our situation tree to come up with a better way of understanding, but we don't exhaustively explore every situation in the tree. We stop as soon as we stumble on the first new set of constraints that will resolve the crux. Such new constraints are better than our old ones, but they themselves may be later superseded by even better constraints as the result of future cruxes.

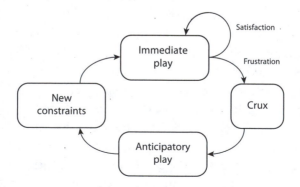

FIGURE 4.2   The cycle of immediate and anticipatory play.

Seen from this perspective, the thresholds that cue intentional shifts from immediate to anticipatory play can be understood as a form of crux. They're a moment when the unfolding of the game takes an unexpected turn, where we move from a known, familiar context to an unknown, unfamiliar one. We pause to reconsider our circumstances, to briefly engage in anticipatory play. Only when our understanding of our new situation has settled into a new set of active constraints do we reenter the moment-to-moment decision-making of immediate play.

In this way, all play experiences consist of an oscillation between satisfaction and frustration, between immediate and anticipatory play. The proportion of time we spend in each type of play depends on the type of game. A Simon-says rhythm game like *Rock Band* mostly consists of immediate play. The right choice in each situation is always clear, and the only cruxes we experience are those caused by the speed and complexity of the patterns exceeding our reflexes. The anticipatory play triggered by these cruxes is very brief, and when it does occur it only produces tiny incremental shifts in our internal constraints—a slight tendency to press the controller buttons earlier or later, or a small improvement in executing common runs of notes.

In contrast, a strategy game like chess consists almost entirely of anticipatory play. Occasionally, our opponent will make a move we expect, and we rapidly follow up with our planned response, but it's far more common for our opponent to surprise us, triggering a crux followed by an extended exploration of the game's changed situation tree. As a result of this elaborated anticipatory play, we may experience sudden large shifts in our internal constraints, adopting entirely new strategies or new ways of understanding our opponent.

A game that consists mostly of immediate play is *doing-directed*. Doing-directed games present us with a continuous stream of low-challenge immediate decisions. Each situation offers a handful of moves, and determining the right move is relatively straightforward. Most moves succeed, and so we constantly experience little bursts of satisfaction. Cruxes are rare, and when they do occur they only produce small shifts in our understanding. The fun of a doing-directed game lies in knowing what to do, and then doing it.

In contrast, a game that consists mostly of anticipatory play is *learning-directed*. Learning-directed games continually present us with situations in which the right move is unclear. They hold still to give us room to engage in elaborated explorations of the situation tree. They often frustrate our expectations, triggering frequent cruxes, and the anticipatory play that follows these cruxes often leads to broad shifts in our understanding. These sweeping readjustments of our internal constraints lead to new strategies and interpretations.

Doing- and learning-directed games both offer valid ways to play. But from a design perspective, it's useful to know where on the doing/learning continuum your game falls. The tension between doing and learning means that different design questions should be addressed in different ways:

	Doing	Learning
Frequency of interaction	High	Low
Chance of frustration	Low	High
Competing goals	No	Yes
Large shifts in understanding	No	Yes
Viable moves per situation	Few	Many

So if you want to create a game that requires the player to discover deep and complicated strategies, keep the frequency of interaction relatively low to allow room for anticipatory play. If you want to create a game that keeps the player continually satisfied with frequent small successes, don't complicate their decision-making process with multiple competing goals. There is no single right answer to questions like, "How hard should a game be?" or "How fast-paced should a game be?" The answers to these sorts of questions always depend on whether the game emphasizes immediate or anticipatory play, and whether it prioritizes doing or learning.

SUMMARY

In immediate play, we pick a move in our current situation, and that move carries us to a new situation that offers us new moves to choose from. In anticipatory play, we roam back and forth through a tree of situations, exploring where different moves lead us. Nevertheless, the situations we encounter within anticipatory play obey the same heuristics as immediate play. They should still offer us choice, variety, consequence, predictability, uncertainty, and satisfaction.

The outcome of anticipatory play is in a shift in our internal constraints—a new plan or prediction that alters our understanding of the game. This shift in our internal constraints changes how we think the game will unfold and what future moves we think we should make as a result. Anticipatory play resolves naturally through closure—we stop exploring the situation tree when we run out of branches to explore and our new understanding settles into a stable state. If anticipatory play needs to be brought to an end before closure is achieved, the transition to immediate play should be foreshadowed so that we can smoothly switch to a different set of active internal constraints.

The transition from immediate to anticipatory play should be cued by a threshold—an abrupt change in context. A threshold is one type of crux. Cruxes occur whenever our expectations are thwarted or our actions fail to achieve their desired effect. They initiate a cascade of anticipatory play, leading to reassessment of our circumstances and our plans. The cycle back and forth between satisfaction and frustration, between immediate and anticipatory play, lies at the core of every play experience.

Depending on the type of play (immediate or anticipatory) that a game prioritizes, we can characterize it as either "doing-directed" or "learning-directed." Both types of games are valid ways to play, but the type of play that a game prioritizes has a powerful effect on many design decisions. Doing-directed games tend to have frequent interactions with a low chance of frustration. They have simple, obvious goals and encourage incremental improvement. Learning-directed games tend to have infrequent interactions with a much higher chance of frustration. They're better at offering multiple layers of competing goals and accommodating large leaps in understanding.

CHAPTER 5

Goals

A GOAL IS A GLOBAL constraint that allows us to distinguish good moves from bad. For example, in chess the goal is to checkmate the enemy king. Any move that advances us toward that state of affairs is a good move, and any move that carries us further away is a bad one. It is the existence of this goal that makes our moves feel consequential. If chess didn't have a goal, then there would be no reason for us to prefer one move over another. All our moves would feel equivalent, and play would collapse.

So, while it may seem as though *we play to win*, it's more accurate to say that *we win to play*. The reason games are winnable is not to reward us, but rather to make our moves feel like they matter. Winning is itself a fleeting experience. We may play a game for many hours, only to be rewarded with a thrill that lasts a few seconds. That one brief moment of triumph doesn't by itself justify the long process of playing. Rather, *the possibility of triumph* creates a bias in the play space, and making moves in accord with this bias makes the game satisfying to play.

This way of thinking about winning has profound design implications. Once we start thinking of goals as tools for constructing consequence, it becomes clear that if the relationship between a game's goals and its situations is missing or obscure, then the choices that we make in those situations will feel pointless. It's not enough for a game to have goals. At every stage of a game, we need to have a sense how our moves make achieving those goals possible.

Furthermore, winning is not the only possible goal. For example, when children play make-believe they're not trying to win. If a child is pretending to be an airplane pilot, there's no specific state of affairs that they're trying to work toward. Their goal is not to beat the other players, but to properly embody the role that they've chosen. So, holding an imaginary control yoke and making motor noises is a good move in a game of "airplane pilot," while growling and running in circles is a bad move. Players in a game of make-believe can clearly distinguish good moves from bad, even though no move is ever directed toward an explicit victory condition.

And even when a game does have an explicit victory condition, we don't always pick moves that advance us toward it. Sometimes, we pick "bad" moves because they make the game more interesting. Or we avoid picking "good" moves because they seem to be cheap or unfair.

If we want to understand why we make the moves we do, we can't limit ourselves to the explicit goals that are stated in the game's rules. We also need to take into account the implicit goals that we bring to the game. Working toward these implicit goals doesn't necessarily help us win; in fact, it often leads to losing. But these implicit goals serve the same purpose as the game's explicit goals. They create a bias in the play space that allows us to distinguish good moves from bad, and so make our actions feel meaningful and consequential.

There are three implicit goals that players bring to every game: *coherence*, *expansion*, and *closure*. Coherence is the sense that we're "getting it right," that the game is going the way that it should, that whatever fantasy the game is creating is being sustained. Expansion is the sense that we're "keeping it interesting," that the game is opening up possibilities at an appropriate pace, and that the situations we encounter are open-ended and challenging. And closure is the sense that we're "accounting for everything," that there are no loose ends or unresolved questions. There's a natural tension between these three implicit goals, and between them and the game's explicit goal (if it has one). Depending on the type of game we're playing, one of these goals might be dominant, but the others are always present, lingering beneath the surface, exerting a subtle tug on every decision we make.

This tension is perhaps easiest to observe in tabletop role-playing games. Unlike traditional board games that primarily focus on winning, role-playing games openly encourage players to use other criteria for determining the worth of a move. Besides trying to stay alive and level up, players are also expected to perform a role and advance the narrative in interesting directions.

So if you're playing a heroic knight you might charge into a battle you know you're certain to lose. You make this "bad" move because it coheres with your fantasy of your character. The move doesn't make sense from the perspective of the explicit goal of "staying alive," but it absolutely supports the implicit goal of "getting it right."

Similarly, if you're playing a bookish monk, your desire to "keep it interesting" might lead you to join up with a band of adventurers in order to explore the local ruins. Staying behind at the monastery to copy a manuscript might be more in character, but such a move doesn't lead to very many interesting situations. Your decision to explore the ruins isn't made because it helps you win, or because it coheres with your fantasy. It's made because it keeps the game interesting.

But there's a limit to how far "keeping it interesting" can take you. Once you set out to explore the local ruins, there's a strong tug to see that particular adventure through to the end. Even though it would be interesting to continually chase after new adventures, there's also a deep satisfaction to completing the adventure you're on. This resolution doesn't have to involve winning, or even be particularly true to your role. Achieving closure is a goal unto itself.

In the rest of this chapter we're going to take a deep look at each of these different implicit goals and explore how they can be used to shape player experience.

COHERENCE PLAY

Coherence play emerges from choosing moves according to how they affect a particular set of privileged internal constraints. These privileged constraints constitute a *role*—a way of being within the game that takes precedence over all other considerations.

When a game is winnable, we try to choose moves that will advance us toward victory. As we proceed from situation to situation, our choices trigger a shift in our internal constraints. Repeated successful moves gradually condense into general strategies, and those strategies change our perception of our future choices. This way of playing treats all our internal constraints as equally malleable. Any move that is allowed by the game's rules is a valid move, and any shift in our internal constraints is permitted.

However, coherence play proceeds from the proposition that some of our internal constraints are off limits to these strategic shifts. When we choose moves in a coherence-oriented game, we're not trying to find the shortest route to some victory condition. We're trying to find the route that minimizes the disruption of these privileged constraints.

So, for example, imagine that you're a child pretending to be a firefighter. There are a large number of moves you can execute from moment to moment, but only a tiny handful of these moves preserve the privileged internal constraint of "act like a firefighter." And out of this handful of moves there are some that do the job better than others. As you proceed from situation to situation you're always trying to discover the move out of this handful that does the best job of reinforcing your privileged internal constraints. Furthermore, because of anticipatory play, you're not just trying to find the one move that does the best job of performing the role of firefighter in the immediate moment. You're also trying to find moves that lead to situations that are ripe with firefighting possibilities.

Good moves in a game of make-believe all "hang together" to sustain a coherent fantasy. Success at make-believe is not a matter of winning, but of "getting it right," so that we feel as though we properly inhabit the role we have chosen. Unlike the explicit goals of winnable games, the coherence goals of make-believe are not terminal. The game doesn't end when we achieve them, the way that a game of chess ends when one king is put in checkmate. The challenge of coherence continues to persist from move to move. Playing make-believe isn't a matter of "getting it right" once. It's a matter of "getting it right" over and over again throughout the play experience. The result is a global bias that allows us to differentiate between good and bad moves without the game having an explicit win state.

Coherence play still obeys the heuristics. Our privileged internal constraints should consistently offer us a small number choices as we advance from situation to situation. In other words, the role we choose to play can't be too narrow or too broad. Pretending to be a firefighter is playful because there are a handful of iconic moves associated with the role to choose from—squirting a hose, chopping down a door, climbing a ladder, rescuing a victim. Narrow roles that require us to do the same thing over and over, or broad roles that are so open-ended they permit almost anything, are much less interesting to play.

The heuristics of variety and consequence also apply to coherence play. The moves we make should carry us to new, unfamiliar situations. Because of this, coherence play works better with roles that involve *doing* more than *being*. A role is defined by the consequential actions that it allows us to perform. Pretending to be a firefighter has more play value than pretending to have blue hair, because the latter doesn't offer us moves that both change our situation and change *with* our situation.

The outcome of our choices in coherence play should be predictable, but not so predictable that we can easily see many moves into the future. This is the reason that playing make-believe becomes less appealing to play as we grow up. An adult can rapidly run through the anticipatory chains implied by a role like "firefighter," exhausting their play potential in a few seconds. But for a child, the outcome of their moves within their role is more uncertain. Free-form coherence play is very hard for a mature player to sustain without other mechanics (dice rolls, other players) to cast a veil over the future.

And finally, coherence play must be satisfying. If we find ourselves in a situation where there aren't any possible moves that will sustain our fantasy, then coherence play will collapse. It's hard to play at being a firefighter if you're sitting in your car seat in the back of a car, for example.

One way to think of coherence play is to picture it taking place within a maze. We adopt a tight set of privileged constraints that severely limit our moment-to-moment moves. The challenge in each situation is not finding the move that helps us win, but finding *any move at all* that doesn't violate our privileged constraints and allows us to keep playing.

Because we're not trying to arrive at any particular state of affairs, there's a natural aimlessness to coherence play. It encourages both exploration and experimentation. We're repeatedly asking ourselves the question, "What would it be like?" What would it be like if I were a firefighter? What would it be like if I were a soldier during the Civil War? What would it be like if I were in command at the Battle of Waterloo? The satisfaction we feel as we explore the maze of privileged constraints comes from our sense that we're answering these questions.

Coherence play is not confined to make-believe. A hard-core historical simulation relies on coherence play just as much a childhood game of pretend. When we play a simulation game, we're often less interested in achieving a particular goal, and more interested in seeing how particular choices play out. Even if the outcome is bad (we lose the battle, our city turns into a slum, our adventuring party is wiped out), there's a playful satisfaction in watching the catastrophe unfold. The "bad" outcome is satisfying because it feels authentic. Our victory comes not from achieving a specific outcome, but from holding true to our privileged constraints and seeing where that fixed strategy takes us.

Furthermore, the role that we perform during coherence play doesn't need to be a fictional one. We all have a sense of who we are as people, and what ethical and personal boundaries we're willing to cross. Coherence play can also be about performing our real-world identities. Sometimes, this performance may be trivial—for example, it might feel subtly satisfying to obey real-world traffic laws in a driving game. The game doesn't require it, but because the role of "good driver" feels comfortable to us, we may unconsciously slip into performing it even though it might not help us win.

But other times, the performance of our identity within a game can be much more fraught. If we're offered an unfair advantage, do we take it? Do we humiliate a weaker opponent? Do we perform actions that, if we did them in the real world, would be morally repugnant? There is a satisfaction to principled play, particularly if sustaining it makes it harder to win. Games can present us with opportunities to act in ways that reinforce our sense of who we are, and these opportunities also represent a form of coherence play.

This sort of identity play is often most obvious when it cuts across the grain of our other goals. For example, a horror game might ask us to perform a morally questionable act in order to escape from danger. The discomfort we feel in such a situation emerges from the tension between our desire to win and our desire to perform an identity that is at odds with what the game is asking of us.

But even when winning aligns with our sense our identity, coherence play can exert a powerful tug. Some games have been described as "power fantasies." A power fantasy is satisfying to play not merely because it lets us win, but because it lets us win in a way that reinforces the self-congratulatory elements of our own identity. In such games we perform the role of the hero, and our victory expresses an identity that is successful and righteous and beloved. The deep satisfaction that comes from winning a power fantasy game comes not just from achieving its explicit goals, but from the correlation of those explicit goals with our own implicit goal of positive identity construction through coherence play.

EXPANSION PLAY

Expansion play emerges from weighing your moves according to how they open up the play space. In each situation, you're not looking for the move that helps you win. You're looking for the move that increases the number of future moves that are available to you. Expansion play requires anticipation. When we engage in anticipatory play, we explore the potential future situations that our moves could lead us to. Each of these future situations will have moves of its own. Some situations will be open—they have a large number of possible moves. Other future situations will be closed—they have few or no moves. In expansion play, we prioritize moves according to whether they lead to more open situations.

Expansion play is sometimes linked to literal exploring: poking around in areas of the map we haven't visited before, trying new moves or tactics or strategies we've previously avoided, playing with an unfamiliar character class or with a different build or load-out. In this case, it's the very unfamiliarity of these situations that makes them feel open. We haven't yet developed the internal constraints that will eventually close off some of these situations' less-valuable moves. So sometimes, expansion play is a deliberate trade-off between victory and variety. We're willing to increase our chances of failure in order to avoid familiar situations that have become played out.

However, expansion play can also lead to choosing familiar situations if we know that those situations offer lots of interesting opportunities to act. For example, in many action games it's possible to avoid enemies simply by running past them. The enemies are tethered to a particular location in the level, and once you get far enough away they'll stop pursuing you. However, even though it may be possible to bypass enemies, most players tend not to. They tend not to because they aren't playing the game to see how quickly they can reach the end of the level. They're playing it to have the experience of heroically defeating their foes.

Running past an encounter is a strategy for winning, while stopping to fight is a strategy for making things interesting. Charging into battle opens up play in a multitude of different ways—there's more to think about, more moves to consider, more to do. Fighting is more interesting than running, and so players are drawn to moves that lead them into fights, regardless of whether or not such a strategy is the most efficient way to achieve the explicit goal of reaching the end of the level alive.

Just as with coherence play, expansion play obeys the heuristics. Even though we're working to maximize our choices, the game should still prevent us from reaching situations where the number of possible moves becomes too large for us to handle. We need to be protected from wandering into a situation so open-ended that it becomes confusing and overwhelming. Open-ended situations shouldn't repeat—in fact, avoiding repetition is particularly important in expansion play because of the need to avoid the constricting effect of learned constraints.

Having predictable consequences is essential if we're going to use anticipation to assess the relative openness of the different moves that are available in our current situation, but at the same time uncertainty about long-term effects can make any move feel much more ambiguous. We should know that we're moving into the unknown. And finally, the game should avoid dead ends. If we're trying to expand our opportunities to act, we shouldn't find ourselves abruptly thwarted.

Designing an expansion game that obeys this final heuristic can be challenging because, after all, games are finite. Exploration and expansion can't be sustained indefinitely; eventually we'll visit most of a game's locations and learn what to do in most of its situations. Providing satisfaction during expansion play is less about creating a game that is endlessly open, but rather about not misleading the player with moves that seem open-ended but actually aren't—for example, an intriguing doorway that leads to an empty room, or a big build-up to a boss battle that is over with a single punch. Routes and choices that imply they lead somewhere interesting should actually pay off in that regard.

Expansion play shares in the aimlessness of coherence play. We don't know exactly where we're headed, but we suspect it will be interesting. But rather than asking ourselves how a particular role will play out, we're motivated purely by a desire to expand our horizons. This means that expansion play often occurs at the expense of coherence. We may break character, go against the grain of our natural tendencies, or reject what is known and comfortable. There is an inherent transgressive element to expansion play, a feeling that we're moving out of bounds.

It is very much the constrained and artificial nature of games that allows this transgression to feel comfortable and desirable. In the real world, movement into the unfamiliar is fraught. The unknown is dangerous, sometimes physically, sometimes emotionally. Open-ended situations with a large variance in outcomes are difficult to navigate. We tend to prefer situations where we know what to do, and our route to success is clear and obvious.

But games provide a walled garden for us to safely act upon our expansive impulses. The stakes in a game are bounded: "It's only a game," we tell ourselves. "The consequences don't really matter." Wandering into the wrong part of a game world won't lead to us being actually humiliated or injured. The worst thing that can happen to us is that we waste a little of our time.

Transgression has its roots in security. Expansion play works best when games reassure us that the negative consequences of choosing poorly are minor. We're more likely to poke around in odd corners of the map if our chances of encountering a dangerous predator are low. We're more likely to attempt an unconventional strategy if our respawn rate is quick. We're more likely to fight a monster just for the fun of it if we're not desperately trying to conserve our health potions.

What this means is that the design of expansion play is not merely a matter of giving players plenty of open-ended situations to choose from. It's also a matter of making sure that the game is not too punishing. (Or that if it is punishing, the punishing elements are clearly segregated from the expansionist ones.) Only when challenges are easy and stakes are low do players feel free to explore situations just for the fun of it.

CLOSURE PLAY

The opposite of expansion play is, of course, closure play. While expansion play is directed toward opening up the possibilities of a play space, closure play is directed toward shutting them down. At first glance this way of playing might seem like it wouldn't be much fun at all. What is the play value of ending a game?

The appeal of closure play lies in the feeling of completeness it provides. *Pokémon* games are advertised with the slogan "Gotta catch 'em all!" and part of the appeal of playing *Pokémon* is the notion that you can, in fact, do just that. Every game in the series contains a few hundred Pokémon for you to catch, and there is a definite satisfaction in trying to collect all of them, even though you know in doing so you're closing off the possibilities of the play space.

Closure play drives us to finish things off, even when finishing them off doesn't help us win or feed into any particular fantasy. It motivates us to collect sets of things, but it also motivates us to wrap up quests and story arcs.

Whether we want our situation to open up or close off depends on where we believe ourselves to be within the game. At the beginning of a gameplay arc, we prefer moves that open up our future possibilities—we play the expansion game. But as the arc draws to a close, we switch goals and prioritize situations that close off possibilities instead. We seek closure. Our movement toward expansion at the beginning and closure at the end operates across all time scales, ranging from the game considered as a whole, to individual quests or stories within the game, to tiny micronarratives consisting of no more than a single isolated encounter or scene.

So when we begin a new game we have a natural bias toward exploration and experimentation, toward pushing the boundaries and doing things purely out of curiosity as to where they will lead. But as we sense that the game is drawing to a close, we turn away from this sort of exploration and concentrate on finishing things off and shutting things down. This process is mirrored at smaller scales within the game—exploration and experimentation when we get a new quest, enter a new level, or face a new encounter, followed by a directed drive toward closure to shut down the opportunities we previously worked to open up.

The use of closure as an implicit goal is closely related to how closure works as an element of anticipatory play. When we want players to stop planning ahead, we encourage them to shift away from anticipatory play by cuing closure. We reduce the number of anticipatory moves available to them, shutting down the anticipatory play space. But players can make the move toward closure themselves without being explicitly steered in that direction. If they're ready for a particular gameplay arc to end, they'll start picking situations to shut it down, even if more open situations are still available to them. They'll ignore side passages, stop talking to quest givers, and stop crafting new gear and instead focus on tying up any lose ends that remain.

Closure play obeys the heuristics. While the danger in expansion play is allowing the player to open the game up so much that it becomes confusing, the danger in closure play is allowing the player to shut the game down too quickly. Endings work best when they feel linear and inevitable, but if an ending becomes too linear we no longer feel like we have any choices to make and play can collapse.

The consequences in closure play should be directed toward closing off avenues of exploration. When we're driven by closure, it's particularly satisfying to make a move that completely shuts down part of the play space: making a one-way jump, knocking an opponent permanently out of the game, collecting the ultimate weapon. Our way forward should be predictable, in the sense that we know whether a move will open up or close off our future options, but not so predictable that we know exactly what form this opening or closing will take. Nevertheless, we should always have the sense that the end is drawing near, that every move we make is narrowing down the game's possibility space until only the final, evitable resolution will remain. We're not trying to "win" in the sense that we achieve a particular conclusion. But we do want to have a sense that the arc we are exploring is resolvable—that there is some possible way to bring it to a satisfying end.

Expansion and closure often conflict with coherence. There's an inherent tension between character and plot, between achieving coherence within an assumed role and managing closure to keep the action moving forward and then resolving. This tension makes the choices within both of these motivational frameworks more interesting. Instead of simply searching through the situation tree to find the single best move in relation to one overriding goal, we often find ourselves with several different "best moves," each one rising to the top within a different intrinsic or extrinsic motivational framework. Do we violate our sense of fairness to pull off a quick, cheap win? Do we reject a solid, boring move to make a more risky (but more interesting) one? Do we turn away from a juicy encounter because it would be out of character? Navigating the tension between these competing goals makes every choice more interesting.

SUMMARY

A goal is a global constraint within a game that allows us to distinguish good moves from bad. Without a way to distinguish good moves from bad, our choices will lack consequence. If any choice is as good as another, then choosing seems pointless, and our feeling of play collapses.

One way to address the need for goals is simply to explicitly state them as part of the game's rules. Many games have an explicit win condition—some privileged situation we're trying to work toward. Any move that advances us toward this privileged situation is a good move, and any move that carries us further away is a bad one.

However, there are other ways besides explicit win conditions to create a feeling of consequence within a game. Players themselves bring implicit goals to every game they play. These implicit goals bias us toward preferring some moves over others, even though they have nothing to do with helping us win:

- The first intrinsic goal is *coherence.* In coherence play, we choose moves according to how well they preserve a fixed set of privileged constraints. Coherence is directed toward "getting it right" and is the primary motivation behind make-believe, role-playing, and hard-core simulation.

- The second intrinsic goal is *expansion*. In expansion play, we choose moves according to how much they open up the game. Expansion is directed toward "keeping it interesting" and is the primary motivation behind exploration, improvisation, and experimentation.

- The third intrinsic goal is *closure*. In closure play, we choose moves according to how much they close off the game. Closure is directed toward "accounting for everything" and is the primary motivation behind collecting, cataloging, and tying up loose ends.

These three intrinsic goals are often in tension with each other, and with the game's explicit goals (if it has them). Our choices within a game are more interesting if they are assigned different values according to different goal frameworks.

CHAPTER 6

Methods

L ET'S RECAP THE MODEL of play we've developed over the previous four chapters.

Our overall sense of the playfulness of a game is a function of the playfulness of its individual situations. Each situation is structured by a collection of constraints. Some of these constraints are external—the game's formal rules, the physics of the play field, the physiology of the players, the programming of the game's software. But most of these constraints are internal—the goals and background knowledge we bring to the game, our functional understanding of the game's external constraints, and the strategies we've learned from playing.

The arrangement of these constraints determines whether or not a situation feels playful. In general, playful situations offer us a handful of moves with predictable consequences. However, we don't engage with these situations in isolation. Our memories of past moves (and how they turned out) act as an internal constraint on our current situation, so if situations repeat they lose their play value. Similarly, if the effects of our moves are too predictable, we can exhaust the play value of future situations before we reach them. And if we can't see a successful way forward from our current situation play will collapse, no matter how well-structured the situation is otherwise.

As we explore these situations, we oscillate between immediate and anticipatory play, between doing and learning. In immediate play, our understanding of the game allows us to quickly pick the best move out the handful that the situation offers. We experience a rush of satisfaction from knowing what to do and doing it. Anticipatory play is more elaborate. If the best move in our current situation isn't obvious, we explore the situation tree containing possible past and future situations. The exploration of this tree is experienced as a flurry of anticipatory moves, each of which contributes to the overall playfulness of the experience. The satisfaction of anticipatory play comes from our sense that our internal constraints have shifted in response to the challenge of the anticipatory play space. We've learned something new about the game.

Anticipatory play is often triggered by a crux. A crux is our sense that our understanding of the game is insufficient for us to make an immediate move in our current situation. This may be because the situation is unfamiliar to us, or because the game unfolded in an unforeseen way, or because a previous move failed to yield the outcome we expected. Anticipatory play always concludes with our internal constraints settling into a new configuration that takes into account the disruption produced by the crux.

In each situation we weigh the value of moves according to our goals. Each goal is an overarching internal constraint that applies to every situation in the game. Goals give us a reason to prefer one move over another, and thus make our choices feel meaningful. Some games have explicit goals—win conditions that are spelled out in their rules. But we also have implicit goals—coherence, expansion, and closure—that affect our choice of moves in both immediate and anticipatory play.

All of these aspects of play—the choices we make according to our various goals, the oscillation between the immediate and the anticipatory, the elaborated exploration of the situation tree, the rapid shifts in our internal constraints that occur as a result—occur far below the level of our conscious awareness. We don't think our way step by step through the process of playing. We're not aware of weighing different alternatives, or considering a multiplicity of hypotheticals. But it is the moment-to-moment quality of this unconscious experience—the degree to which each situation aligns with the heuristics of play—that determines whether or not we find an experience playful, or satisfying, or meaningful.

This model of play yields a design methodology—a way to reason our way through design problems. This methodology takes the player's experience as its starting point. Rather than trying to come up with a game system that is playable in the abstract, we start out by identifying an experience that we want the player to have. Are they supposed to feel large and powerful, or small and fearful? Are they supposed to feel like a highly respected member of a tightly knit team, or a shunned loner doing a thankless job? Are they supposed to feel proud of their actions during the game? Ashamed? Ambivalent? When the game is over, do we want them to feel pleased with themselves and triumphant? Or anxious and disturbed?

If we know the intended experience, we can then block out a representative set of performative moves that encapsulate that experience. And if we know the sorts of performative moves that we want the player to make, then we can use the heuristics of play to design typical situations in which those moves will emerge playfully from the choices presented to the player. Knowing the situations that we want to put the player in tells us the sorts of constraints that we need to impose upon them. And once we know the constraints that the player needs to possess, we can design a system that either imposes them directly, or that cues their adoption as part of the Game as Understood. This system is the game we design (Figure 6.1).

This methodology applies to subsystems within a game as well as the game as a whole. We can use it to design an inventory system, or a traversal mechanic, or a boss battle. We always start with an experience we want the player to have, identify moves that express that experience, figure out playful situations that will structure those moves, determine the

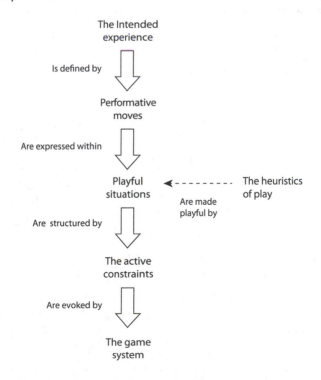

FIGURE 6.1 Situational game design methodology.

constraints we need to create those situations, and then design a subsystem that will evoke those constraints.

While this process is presented as a strict cascade, in practice it will inevitably unfold in a way that is iterative and recursive, with frequent false starts and backtracks. Our understanding of the experience we want to create for the player may shift as we experiment with different moves, situations, and constraints. The system we actually design may yield unexpected pockets of play, or allow moves that we didn't anticipate when we first began planning it. These deviations from formalism should be welcomed, not discouraged. The methodology is a lens to help us focus our creativity, not a straightjacket to prevent us from exploring interesting avenues of play when we discover them.

DESIGNING MOVES

The moves that we make as we play are a performance. They define a way of being within the world of the game, and so they form the thread from which the fabric of our experience is woven. So, our first step when we set out to design an experience is always to ask ourselves this: What does the player *do*?

The design of moves should be fine-grained and specific. So, for example, it's not enough to say, "The player fights against monsters!" We need to actually think through the specific combat moves that are in the player's palette. Are they fast and sloppy? Slow and deliberate? Is there a block move or a dodge? Does each move stand alone, or can they be chained together in combos? Each of these choices contributes to the texture of the combat experience and to the role the player performs while they're immersed within it.

When blocking out a provisional move set, there are a variety of factors to keep in mind. The most basic is the physicality of the control inputs. *Rock Band* is more than a just a Simon-says game because the physicality of the custom guitar controller encourages us to mimic a rock star as we play. This same performative physicality also affects games with more mundane controllers. Pressing a button, moving a mouse, or swiping across a touch screen are embodied acts. Pulling a trigger creates an increase in the tension of our hands, while releasing a trigger has the opposite effect. Charging an attack by holding a button down feels different from charging an attack by rapidly tapping. Swiping away from us feels different than swiping toward us. If we think of making a move as performing a role, then the tactile sensation of triggering it contributes to the role that we're performing.

Closely related to the physicality of moves is their cadence. The pacing of moves is not merely a matter of difficulty (although, obviously that plays a factor) but of performance. Asking the player to make a number of moves in rapid succession creates a feeling of urgency or panic. The same moves spread out over a longer time frame can convey deliberation or calm. One of the key design elements in the original *Rainbow Six* was a targeting reticle that rewarded players for taking slow, deliberate shots. Rapidly spraying bullets in all directions was designed to be a losing strategy, and it was designed to be a losing strategy because maintaining a slow, deliberate cadence contributed to the feeling that your character was cool-headed and methodical.

The context and consequence of a move also affects its performative significance. Swinging a sword at an empty crate is a different experience than swinging a sword at a charging knight. So when we block out an experience we're not merely compiling a list of actions, we're also thinking about the circumstances that will bring those actions into active consideration. Why would a player make such a move? What does the move accomplish within the game? A move is not merely a thing that the player does at random; players make moves for reasons. A move is a thing that does something meaningful within the context of the game, and the significance we attach to it is tightly bound to the performative work we think it's doing.

By considering the consequences of different moves, we're edging into the next step of the methodology: the design of playful situations. And indeed, our job in the next step will be easier if we keep the heuristics of play in mind as we sketch out our moves. So moves should be designed have distinct and predictable consequence. They should change the internal or external state of the game in meaningful ways, and different moves should have different effects. Don't give the player two ways to accomplish the same thing. Each alternative within the player's range of actions should lead to a different trajectory through the play space, and the player should be able to anticipate (at least roughly) what that trajectory will be.

Moves are not directed only toward the external state of the game, but also to the player's own internal conceptions. Performative moves are not just what the player actively does; they're also what they're thinking about. So, "wondering which way to go" is a performative move, as is, "feeling guilty over a previous encounter." In blocking out a palette of moves, we also need to take into account moves that exist entirely within anticipatory or interpretive play. The more strategic and introspective a game is, the more attention we need to pay to designing for these sorts of non-interactive moves.

Ultimately, the goal in this step of the methodology is to build up a specific sense of what it means from moment to moment for the player to inhabit their intended role within the game. What do we want them to be thinking about? And what do we want them to be doing? And how does this thinking and doing change their understanding of the game or their circumstances within it in significant ways?

DESIGNING SITUATIONS AND CONSTRAINTS

Merely because a collection of moves describes a coherent role within a game, that doesn't mean enacting that role will necessarily feel playful. The playfulness of the role depends upon how those moves are organized into particular situations, and how those situations obey the heuristics of play.

Once we've defined an intended experience by blocking out the sorts of moves we'd like the player to perform, we then need to design representative situations that will allow those moves to be expressed. This means closely analyzing the moment-to-moment decisions we want the player to make, and constructing active constraints that provide the necessary affordances.

Often this step is relatively straightforward. For example, if we want to give the player the experience of being a heroic knight, then this step involves the creation of challenging monsters and scenarios for monster-killing. We can break down each encounter into clusters of immediate and anticipatory situations and analyze how well each of them satisfies the heuristics of play: How many moment-to-moment choices are we giving the player? Are we varying them so they don't get played out? Are their consequences predictable enough that choosing has a sense of agency? Are they so predictable that their play value can be prematurely exhausted? Can players see their way through to a satisfying outcome?

What makes this process challenging is that we never have complete control over the constraints that structure the situations that we're designing. Merely because we write a rule, or build a level, or place an enemy, we can't be certain that the player will understand those constraints in exactly the way that we intended. We can't take for granted that the Game as Understood is equivalent to the Game as Designed.

For this reason, we need to adopt of the notion of the *assumed player* when designing gameplay situations. The assumed player is a hypothetical player who possesses the proper internal constraints to complete the externally structured situations and make them playable. Situations never satisfy the heuristics in isolation; they do so by being paired with the appropriate assumed player.

Every situation is designed for some assumed player, whether we consciously realize it or not. If we don't make a point of explicitly considering the assumptions we're making about who is playing, then we're likely to unconsciously design situations with ourselves as the assumed player— the assumed player becomes someone who shares our background and biases and knowledge. Or we're likely to unconsciously design situations for an omniscient assumed player—the assumed player becomes someone who possesses all possible knowledge of the game and its context.

The construction of a hypothetical assumed player is difficult. We have to imagine what it's like to play through the situations we create knowing *less* than we know. Or, even more difficult, we have to imagine what it's like to play through the situations we create knowing *more* than we know, or *different things* than we know. This is why playtesting is so important at later stages of a project—it brings actual players who may deviate from our assumptions in contact with the game.

(There are several corollaries of this observation. The first is that one of the most important things you can do during playtesting is figure out why a tester made an unexpected move. At the time it happened, what internal model did the tester possess of the game, and how can that information be used to adjust your model of the assumed player?

The second corollary is the value of collaboration and diversity in design. The members of the development team themselves represent a collection of different possible players with different backgrounds and experiences. This means that different members of the team will have different insights into what makes the situations we create playful and satisfying, and the wider those differences are—whether cultural, or gendered, or circumstantial—the better we can anticipate the sorts of rules we need to write to make our situations playful.)

Contained within the assumed player are assumptions about their motivations. If our game is winnable, we can usually take it as a given that most players will choose their moves according to whether or not they help them win. However, even when a game has explicit win conditions, it's often useful to consider alternate assumed players with other motivations. Trolls and griefers, for example, may ignore the game's explicit goals and instead engage in a form of expansion play where they choose moves according to the emotional reactions they trigger in other players. For these players, a move that gets an interesting reaction is better than one that leads to victory.

The motivations of the assumed player become even more important when we design games that don't have explicit win conditions. Because the player must supply their own criteria for distinguishing good moves from bad, such a game can fail completely if the player approaches it with the wrong attitude. For example, "walking simulators" can be powerful and moving experiences for players who approach them as performances or narratives, but can seem empty and pointless to players who are unwilling to engage in coherence, expansion, or closure play. The problem is not that the game itself is inherently unplayful, but rather that some players don't approach them with the necessary internal constraints to structure a viable play space. The distance between this category of actual player and the game's assumed player is too great.

When we design games without explicit win conditions, we need to be particularly sensitive to what we're expecting from our assumed player. What motivations should a player possess in order to engage successfully with the situations that we're designing? How can we signal to the player the attitude that the game expects from them? To some extent this can be accomplished by how the experience is framed. Labeling something "an interactive experience" rather than "a game" suggests that it requires a strategy of engagement other than playing to win.

But the adoption of implicit goals can also be triggered by providing early explicit rewards for successful coherence, expansion, or closure play. Small explicit goals can be used to train the player to use implicit criteria to determine the worth of moves. For example, if we want the player to explore, we can hide small rewards in easy-to-find places around the starting area. Finding these small rewards can prime the player to adopt the implicit goal of expansion, which can then sustain a tendency toward exploration even if the explicit rewards become more infrequent as the game progresses.

DESIGNING GAMES

Players don't play the Game as Designed; they play the Game as Understood. So when we set out to design situations or constraints for the player to play within, we must do so indirectly. We don't design the actual situations or constraints they'll use to play. Rather, we design a system that's capable of evoking those situations or constraints in the player's mind when they engage with it.

For example, enemy characters are often designed to behave in ways that encourage the player to regard them as human beings. This cues the player to call up a wide variety of behavioral constraints that they've learned from a lifetime of dealing with other humans. The player doesn't learn the coded rules of the game's AI. Rather, they substitute a functionally similar collection of pre-existing constraints. The player doesn't play against the enemies as they are, but rather a version of the enemies that they cobble together from their existing understanding of real-world humans and enemies they've encountered in other games.

Every player, whether actual or assumed, begins a game with a *conceptual background*. The conceptual background is the prior knowledge that the player brings to the game. This knowledge may come from real-world experiences or from other similar games. If we start to play a new driving game, we already have an unconscious sense of how the car should handle based on our experience with real-world cars and other driving games. This unconscious sense will affect what we attempt to do. Before we make our first move there are already things we think we can do and things we think we can't.

Based on the way the game responds to our moves—the expectations that it satisfies and the cruxes that we encounter—our initial conceptual background evolves into a *functional understanding* of the Game as Experienced. This functional understanding is a system of internal constraints that allows us to pick good moves and make accurate predictions about how the game is likely to unfold. Eventually, if we play the game long enough, this functional understanding will broaden into a collection of *deep strategies*. These strategies are not a functional description of how the game behaves, but rather a set of constraints that we can rely on to guide us to success in a wide variety of situations.

While these strategies are related to the Game as Designed, they don't recapitulate any part of it. For example, "control the center" is a useful strategy in chess, but chess doesn't have any specific rules that reward the player for controlling the center. The strategies we learn when we become experts at a game are not "contained" within their external structure, but are inventions that we create in response to it. And, indeed, the particular strategies we invent to cope with a game may not be what the designer intended, or even imagined.

This progression—from a provisional understanding cobbled together from the player's conceptual background, to a functional understanding of the game's behavior based on played experience, to a collection of deep strategies that float unmoored from the game's structure—is how the Game as Understood naturally evolves. What this means is that the assumed player is not a static entity. And when we design a system of rules, we're not creating just one game. We're creating an unfolding multiplicity of games. When players start to play, their conceptual background *is* the Game as Understood. But as they move from situation to situation, their internal constraints shift and adapt in response to the expectations they form and the cruxes they experience. New functional understandings and deep strategies gradually emerge (Figure 6.2).

So rather than thinking of the Game as Designed as a playable system in its own right, it's often more useful to think of the Game as Designed simply as a system for triggering shifts in the system that is actually being played—the Game as Understood. The game we design exists primarily as a mechanism for continually nudging the player's internal constraints into a succession of playful configurations.

For example, consider something as simple as corner geometry in level design. In general, hard corners tend to be more playful than soft corners because of the effect they have on the player's perception of choice. Prior

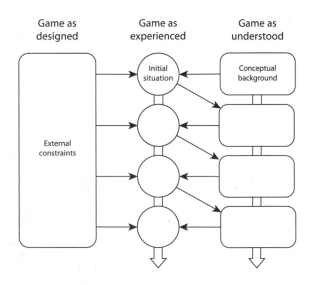

FIGURE 6.2 A multiplicity of understood games.

to arriving at both types of corner, the player is in the dark about what lies ahead, which gives them the opportunity to engage in a bit of anticipatory play. When they turn a hard corner a new context is revealed abruptly, with all its potentialities exposed simultaneously. Turning a hard corner creates a playful situation because it offers the player an interesting range of new choices.

However, turning a soft corner doesn't structure the same playful situation. When the player turns a soft corner, the reveal is gradual, so the sense of having a range of new choices is reduced. From a purely mechanical perspective within the Game as Designed, the two types of corner offer the same opportunities for player action. But because they create different perceptions of choice within the Game as Understood, they play very differently. The design of the corner determines whether or not the player's understanding is nudged toward a playful configuration. The layout of the level affects what the player knows, and what the player knows affects how the level plays.

There are a variety of techniques that a game can use to evoke particular active constraints in the mind of the player:

- *Reveals*: Choices only matter when we're aware of them. A game can hide certain choices from us to keep us from becoming overwhelmed, or make sure (as with a hard corner) that different moves are framed in a way that makes the choice between them clear.

- *Cues*: The way that game entities are presented will suggest which constraints we should borrow from our conceptual background. If a guard looks alert, we'll play more cautiously, regardless of whether that alertness is reflected in the guard's coded behavior.

- *Feedback*: How the game communicates the effects of a move affects our functional understanding of it. If a weapon hit knocks over nearby tables and chairs, we'll assume it has blast damage.

- *Coincidences*: The circumstances of a crux affect how we resolve it. If an attack fails when an enemy dodges, we'll assume the failure was caused by the dodge.

- *Goals*: If we believe a particular game state represents a goal, we'll move toward it. If we believe that hidden rewards might be scattered around a level, we'll look around to find them, whether they're actually there or not.

The guiding principle to situational design is to focus on what the player believes about the game, rather than on the game itself. We establish an early model of what the player believes by constructing an assumed player with an initial set of internal constraints drawn from their conceptual background. We then "walk" the assumed player through a series of conceptual shifts triggered by the cruxes they encounter as they play the game.

What this means, ideally, is that the system of the game responds to the evolving state of the assumed player—that the external constraints that the game currently provides are the right ones to intersect with the internal constraints that the player currently possesses to structure a playful experience.

At its most basic, this responsiveness may simply be grounded in player progression. If the player is able to defeat the first boss, that tells us something about their understanding of the game, and so the situations that we structure after the first boss can be constructed around a version of the assumed player that takes that understanding into account.

Seen from this perspective the standard gating mechanics we see in many games—locked levels, escalating enemies, expert move sets—aren't there just to give players a feeling of accomplishment. They're also a design tool, a way to give designers a handle on the unruly assumed player. We can't know everything that an individual player will bring to a play experience, but, if we include a hard gate in the game's progression that gives us a clue as to the sorts of internal constraints that the player likely possesses after they pass through it.

However, a deeper and more difficult type of system-level responsiveness is to look at player behavior as a clue to player belief and intent. For example, the scariness of a horror game depends a great deal on the attitude of the player toward the game. Ideally, the player should be in a state of apprehension, creeping nervously forward, worried about what's around every corner.

If a player doesn't approach the game with this mindset, it won't be as scary. So, one technique in the design of horror games is to build in harsh penalties if the player fails to properly perform the role of terrorized victim. If the player boldly runs everywhere and throws doors open at random, then they're punished with jump scares and brutal deaths. The penalties aren't there because they're fun in and of themselves, or because they're particularly challenging to avoid. They're there to nudge the player's internal constraints into alignment with the internal constraints of the assumed player that the game was designed for. Certain player behaviors are evidence that the player possesses certain beliefs and intentions, and the game can respond accordingly.

SUMMARY

Situational game design is a player-centric methodology for creating games. It starts with the experience that the game is intended to provide: What role should the player perform as they play the game? From the player's intended role we can then design a set of performative moves—a set of actions and contexts that embody the experience the game is intended to deliver.

These performative moves are organized into playful situations using the heuristics of play—choice, variety, consequence, predictability, uncertainty, and satisfaction. In order to construct these situations, we must first construct an assumed player. The assumed player models the internal constraints that a typical player brings to the game—their conceptual background, their functional understanding, and their deep strategies.

Once we block out our desired situations, we can then design a game system capable of evoking them. This system operates not by imposing its constraints directly, but by indirectly triggering them in the mind of the assumed player. The adoption of these new internal constraints is governed by how the game presents new information, and how it responds to cruxes.

Such a game system is not playable in its own right. Rather, it's a mechanism for continually nudging the player's internal constraints into a succession of playful configurations. When we design a system of rules, we're not creating just one game. We're creating an unfolding multiplicity.

CHAPTER 7

Narrative

O NE ADVANTAGE OF THE situational approach to game design is that it allows us to put gameplay and story on the same footing. The game's rules and our attitudes toward those rules form a system of constraints, and the playfulness of the situations that those constraints structure determines the overall quality of the game. However, the various elements of the game's story—its settings, its characters, its scenes, and its incidents—also form a system of constraints. Those narrative elements, along with our evolving attitudes toward the story, also structure a succession of situations, or *story beats*, and the playfulness of these story beats can also be analyzed using the same heuristics of play.

By erasing the analytical distinction between game elements and story elements, we can create a more seamless fusion of the two into a unified experience. Situational design gives us a way to understand game mechanics as story mechanics and vice versa. The role that we perform as we move from situation to situation during gameplay becomes a character within our evolving understanding of the story. And the incidents that occur within the story become constraints on the moves we make during gameplay.

The notion of narrative play may seem at odds with the conventional wisdom about how stories work. After all, stories are linear and non-interactive. They consist of a fixed set of characters that proceed through an inevitable series of incidents. The ending of a story is determined in advance, and there's nothing we can do as readers to change it, or even to introduce the slightest swerve in the author's intended narrative trajectory.

And yet, within this rigid structure, the reader still retains a considerable amount of agency. We may not have any control over what happens within a story, but we have a great deal of control over how we interpret it. Two readers can read exactly the same story and yet come away with profoundly different senses of what it means. Much of the study of literature is an argument over the correct way to interpret a story. What distinguishes a good interpretation from a bad one? How can we learn to interpret texts that at first glance seem flat or impenetrable?

The play that we experience when we engage with a story is similar to anticipatory gameplay. We're not making moves that change the external game—we're making moves that change our internal system of constraints. We're constructing interpretations and expectations that will later be either confirmed or falsified by future story beats.

We don't "win" a story in the sense that we discover a way to reach a particular privileged situation. We can't control what the story's ending is, or even force ourselves to assign it a particular meaning. However, the implicit goals of coherence, expansion, and closure give us a way to distinguish good interpretive moves from bad ones. Satisfying narrative play is not a matter of steering either the story itself or our interpretation of it in a particular direction, but rather of repeatedly encountering story beats that present us with interpretive moves that are challenging to choose between.

NARRATIVE CONSTRAINTS AND SITUATIONS

In order to understand how narrative play works, we first need to understand what sorts of constraints structure the narrative play space. The most obvious constraint in narrative play is the text. If we're reading a book, the text consists of the words on the page. If we're watching a movie the text consists of the images on the screen and the dialog and music that we hear. If we're playing a videogame the text consists of the cinematics we watch, the characters we interact with, the mission briefings we read—all the assorted bits and pieces of story information embedded within the experience.

However, the text is not the only constraint structuring the situations we encounter. In addition to the story's overt text, there is also its *paratext*, the context in which it's presented. A book's paratext includes its cover art, the advertising blurbs on its dust jacket, its typeface, the physicality of its pages. A video game's paratext includes its box art, the quality of the screen that it's played on, the trailers that were used to advertise it. All of these minor elements affect how we interpret the text in subtle ways, biasing us toward or against particular ways of engaging.

More significant than the paratext is our own conceptual background. When we engage with a story, even a very simple one, most of the constraints we draw on to make sense of it come from our own experiences with real life or other stories. We know how human beings behave, and we know how particular situations are likely to unfold, and it is these internal constraints that allow us to navigate the unfolding narrative, forming expectations about where it's headed and what it signifies.

These *extratextual constraints* arise from a variety of sources:

- *Canon*: We carry with us a warehouse of interpretive strategies we've learned from engaging with other texts. If a character announces they're worried about something, we know from our prior experience with other stories that their worries are likely to be significant to the plot.

- *Genre*: The type of story we think we're reading affects how we read it. If we think we're reading a romance, we expect that the main character will, no matter what, eventually wind up with their love interest, and this affects how we interpret various situations.

- *Culture*: Each of us is embedded within particular historical, social, cultural, political, and economic circumstances. These circumstances create normative assumptions that influence our interpretation of a work.

- *Apocrypha*: Difficult texts can be made accessible by supporting documentation. If we're struggling to engage with an eighteenth-century novel, we may need commentary to help us make sense of passages that are rendered opaque by their unfamiliar cultural context.

- *Life*: Each of us has our own lived experiences. The death of a parent, the fear of being bullied—our knowledge and memories of these past events has a profound effect on how we interpret story beats.

Taken together, these textual and extratextual constraints structure a series of situations as the story unfolds. As we proceed through the story, the textual constraints are constantly changing; each successive word that we read on the page (or each successive image that appears on the screen) creates new interpretive possibilities. But our internal constraints are constantly changing as well, shifting and flowing as we attempt to make sense of the unfolding text.

A narrative beat is a situation within a story that structures an interpretive choice. When we're within a narrative beat, our active textual and extratextual constraints allow us a handful of possible interpretive moves. For example, say the words on the page tell us a stranger appears on the road ahead. What is this figure's significance to the story? Our minds race up and down the narrative situation tree, forming hypotheses and testing them against what we already know about the story and the world. Within a fraction of a second we settle on an interpretation: The stranger is a bandit waiting to ambush our hero! But as soon as that provisional interpretation forms in our mind, it's already being reconsidered in light of the words that follow. We discover that the stranger is well-dressed and has a friendly face. Is that evidence against him being a bandit, or evidence in favor of him being a particularly cunning one? And so the interpretive process begins anew.

A story consists of a series of narrative beats (Figure 7.1). Each beat offers us a choice of interpretive moves. Each move represents a shift in the internal constraints that constitute our understanding of the story. This understanding not only accounts for the beats that come before, but structures an expectation of what will follow.

Our anticipation of what lies ahead drifts and wanders as we encounter each new beat (Figure 7.2). So as we read a story (or watch it, or listen to it) our sense of where it's headed is constantly changing. We think we know what's going on, but we don't know for sure, and that uncertainty allows

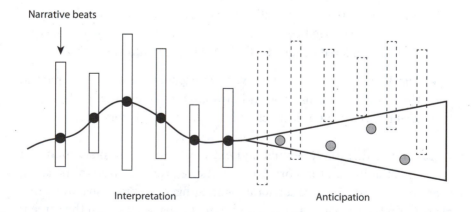

Narrative beats

Interpretation   Anticipation

FIGURE 7.1   A series of narrative beats.

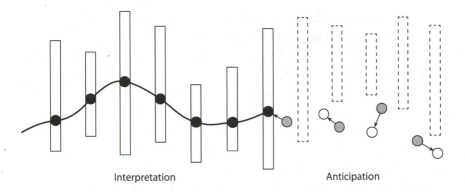

Interpretation   Anticipation

FIGURE 7.2   Wandering anticipation.

us to continually rewrite our expectations in response the changing constraints imposed by the text.

Most of the time, as we move through a story, our expectations are satisfied. We believe the narrative will unfold in a particular way, and so, when the text confirms our expectations were correct, we experience a little rush of satisfaction. We understand what's going on, and that understanding has allowed us to correctly predict the story's trajectory. However, sometimes the story swerves in an unexpected direction. We thought we knew what was going to happen, but something else happened instead. This moment is a crux. A crux doesn't just trigger a shift in our expectations. It triggers a shift in the interpretations that allowed us to form those expectations. When we experience a narrative crux, our minds race backward through previous story beats, adjusting our prior interpretations to account for the unexpected beat we've just encountered (Figure 7.3).

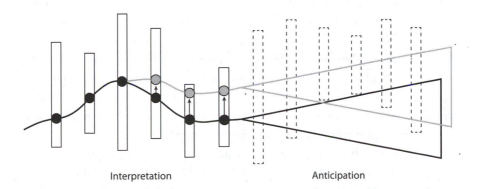

Interpretation   Anticipation

FIGURE 7.3   Resolving a crux.

This is the basic situational model for how we experience narrative. The text is a system of constraints. As we move forward through the text we encounter ambiguous narrative situations—story beats—that invite an interpretive move. By settling on an interpretation of these beats, we form an expectation of what beats we will encounter in the future. If the text meets our expectations then we experience a brief burst of satisfaction and refine our anticipation of the future. But if the text thwarts our expectations, then we experience a crux and retroactively adjust our interpretations to account for the discontinuity.

This is how narrative reception can be both playful and active, despite the fact that it is both deterministic and non-interactive. We continually range backward and forward within the possibility space structured by the constraints of the text. However, the moves that we make are entirely internal. They have no effect on the static external structure of the story, but they have a profound effect on the system of internal constraints that represent our understanding of it.

NARRATIVE PLAY

This back-and-forth movement through the constraints of the text happens whenever we try to make sense of a narrative. However, in order for this movement to be enjoyable, the beats that we encounter during this process need to obey the heuristics of play. It's not enough merely to pile up textual constraints haphazardly. The constraints need to offer us choice, variety, consequence, predictability, uncertainty, and satisfaction in order for the story as a whole to feel playful and engaging.

Choice is the most basic requirement. A beat must contain some degree of ambiguity to feel playful. If the meaning of a beat is completely obvious then it won't provide any narrative play. Of course, sometimes we want our communications to be as precise and unambiguous as possible. If we're reading an instruction manual then we want the meaning of each sentence to be obvious. We don't read an instruction manual for its own sake—we read it because we want to know how to operate the device it explains. An instruction manual doesn't need to be engaging or entertaining. And, in fact, since ambiguity is one of things that make a text engaging, making an instruction manual entertaining may actually work against the precision that is so important to its primary purpose.

But stories are different. We consume stories for their own sake because we want to have the experience of playfully engaging with them. And so they need to tease and beguile us by deliberately leaving some things uncertain or unsaid. If a story consists of nothing but blunt declarations of fact that offer little room for interpretation, it quickly becomes boring. Each beat needs to offer us a collection of interpretative moves—a range of different ways for us to shift our understanding to account for it.

However, at the same time this ambiguity needs to be bounded. If a beat is too open-ended, if there are too many different ways to interpret it, then our resulting confusion will cause play to collapse. Just as with gameplay situations, narrative situations work best when they offer us a handful of viable alternatives to consider. A beat that can be interpreted in five different ways is more playful than a beat with dozens of different interpretations.

Note that the interpretive moves we can make within a beat are not limited simply to deciding what's going on. Narrative ambiguity is not simply a matter of keeping the reader off balance with continual twists and surprises. There are a number of other types of ambiguity that readers can play with:

- *Grammatical*: What does this word mean in this context?

- *Syntactical*: How should I interpret this sentence?

- *Motivational*: What is this character trying to accomplish?

- *Logistical*: What just happened?

- *Thematic*: What is this story about?

- *Contextual*: Why did the author write this?

Most stories wander between these (and other) types of ambiguity as they proceed from beat to beat. The particular type of interpretive choice is less important than the fact that there *are* interpretive choices. A story beat is only playful if it poses a question with a small number of possible answers.

It should go without saying, but our individual extratextual constraints have a large effect on how much ambiguity a beat possesses. If we don't know anything about nineteenth-century English social mores, then we'll likely be confused by the apparently unbounded interpretive choices offered by a period comedy of manners. By the same token, if a story is too formulaic and clichéd, we may find ourselves bored by it. The answers to its interpretive questions are so obvious that they don't feel like choices.

We experience a similar sort of boredom when story beats repeat themselves. An interpretive choice only feels like a choice the first time we encounter it. If we're presented with the same choice again, we remember our previous interpretive moves, and so the situation no longer feels playful.

This is the heuristic of variety. In narrative terms, it means avoiding redundant exposition or exhaustive elaboration. Repetitive beats may seem to offer interpretive choices, but because these choices involve matters that are already played out, they don't engage us. Successive beats should always give us new ambiguities to consider. As soon as we we've converged on a fixed interpretation of an incident, a character, or a theme, the story needs to move on, either by triggering a crux in our existing understanding through the introduction of new, contradictory textual constraints, or by opening up a new field of narrative play through the introduction of fresh incidents, characters, or themes.

Each story beat should offer a new interpretive choice, and these interpretive choices must build on each other and grow as the story progresses. It's not interesting to be told the same thing over and over again—that the villain secretly admires the hero, for example. We either need for their relationship to evolve so that we have new decisions to make, or the story needs to take this aspect of their relationship as a given and offer us a different ambiguity to explore.

Because we remember our interpretive choices, these choices should not just demonstrate variety, they should also be consequential. In other words, any decision that we make to resolve the ambiguity of our current beat should form a meaningful constraint on future beats. If we decide that the villain secretly admires the hero, that's an interesting interpretive move because it colors our perception of every interaction between them going forward. Such an interpretive move feels meaningful and significant when we make it. We've uncovered something big and important that profoundly affects the course of our future narrative play.

Beats that don't have any long-term effect on the course of the narrative are *gratuitous*. A trivial interaction that doesn't affect our understanding of the main characters, a subplot that never goes anywhere, a conflict that doesn't move the action forward—all of these gratuitous situations may seem playful when we first encounter them, but because the decisions we make as we resolve them don't have any consequences for the rest of the narrative, the moves we make in response to them feel empty and pointless.

In order for us to perceive that an interpretive move is consequential, we need to be able to predict its likely consequences. A quarrel between the protagonist and her best friend will be more engaging than a quarrel between the protagonist and a random bystander. It's more engaging because the quarrel with the best friend can trigger a long chain of hypothetical events. How will it affect future interactions between them? Will it lead to an eventual reconciliation or a permanent estrangement? The interpretive moves we make in such a situation feel consequential because we can predict what those consequences are likely to be.

On the other hand, if the protagonist gets in a quarrel with a random bystander, we have a much harder time envisioning where it's headed. Because the bystander doesn't seem connected to the overall story, we can't predict where the quarrel will lead and how choosing a particular interpretation of the incident will affect future beats. Lack of predictability leads to lack of consequence. The quarrel feels pointless and gratuitous, and won't provide much narrative play.

Often, a lack of predictability is perceived as a plot hole. The text tells us that something has happened, but the incident doesn't feel connected to previous events in the narrative and to our general understanding of what's going on. We can't reconcile our previous sense of where the story was headed with the new information that the text has provided.

In practice, we tend to extend authors a great deal of leeway when it comes to presuming significance. If we don't know at first how a character or an incident connects to the future unfolding of the narrative, we'll often give the author the benefit of the doubt and invent an interpretation that imbues an apparently inconsequential situation with long-term consequence. So rather than immediately losing interest because the quarrelsome bystander seems unimportant, we'll instead start looking for ways to fit the bystander into the plot. Our first impulse is to trust the author and assume that if the narrative contains an incident, it's because that incident is somehow important.

This is the source of Chekhov's Gun. In playwright Anton Chekhov's own words, "One must never place a loaded rifle on the stage if it isn't going to go off. It's wrong to make promises you don't mean to keep." The audience will presume every incident structured by the text is significant. If at first we can't predict the effects of an interpretive choice, we will invent additional constraints to allow us make predictions. And these additional constraints have the capacity to significantly warp our unfolding understanding of the narrative. We will be continually distracted by the rifle on the stage, repeatedly trying to work it into a version of the story that the text itself will never deliver on. We need to be able to perceive the significance of our narrative choices, and if the text doesn't overtly supply that significance, we are likely to invent a significance of our own.

However, while we should be able to perceive the significance of our choices, our predictions can't be so obvious and all-encompassing that they preempt all future ambiguities. If we know exactly how the story is going to unfold, then there's no longer any reason for us to keep engaging with it. The text no longer offers us any surprises or choices to make and its playfulness collapses.

So a story should always preserve some element of uncertainty. We might think we know where it's headed and why particular interpretive choices matter. But we're never quite sure that our whole careful edifice of understanding won't be upended by some unexpected twist or revelation. The ending is always in doubt, right up until we read the final word on the final page.

And, finally, there is the heuristic of satisfaction. This doesn't mean that the stories have to turn out the way we want them to, or even that we should be able to choose an interpretation we want. Rather, it means that we are consistently able to find interpretive moves that satisfy the implicit goals of coherence, expansion, and closure.

When we interpret a story beat, we try to do so in a way that minimizes the disruption of the existing constraints that we have built up in response to previous beats. So, if, for example, we're trying to understand a character's motivations, we try to do so in a way that coheres with our existing understanding of the character. If a character behaves in ways that are radically inconsistent from one scene to the next, then we won't be able to find an interpretive move that preserves coherence. A story may obey all the other heuristics, but if successive beats repeatedly fail to cohere with each other, then the experience of navigating it won't feel satisfying.

Similarly, if we're near the beginning of a story, we seek out interpretive moves that open up the story's possibility space. We tend to reject mundane interpretations in favor of more fantastic ones. So if the protagonist discovers an old key, we start imagining all the exciting secrets that the key might unlock. We don't assume that the key unlocks their front door, even though that's a perfectly reasonable assumption. In order for us to experience satisfaction near the beginning of a story, the beats we encounter need to present the possibility of expansion. They need to offer interpretative moves that open up new vistas for us to explore.

When we reach the end of a story, the opposite is true. We want to find moves that shut down avenues of anticipatory play. This means that ending story beats should provide us with the opportunity to conclude story arcs, resolve character conflicts, and tie up loose ends. In order for us to experience satisfaction near the end of a story, the beats we encounter need to present the possibility of closure. They need to offer interpretive moves that close off the narrative play space.

If we treat story beats as situations, the heuristics of play become a set of general rules for how stories should be structured so that they will feel playful and interesting when we engage with them (Table 7.1).

Our application of the heuristics of narrative resembles the storytelling rules that are taught to beginning writers. The heuristics don't tell us anything unexpected about what makes a story engaging. Rules like "don't write in clichés" or "avoid plot holes" or "tie up loose ends" are widely known. Rather, the heuristics explain *why* these storytelling rules exist in the first place. They exist because a good narrative creates an interpretive play space and violating these simple rules interferes with interpretive play.

TABLE 7.1 Narrative Heuristics

Heuristic	General Principle	Narrative Application
Choice	Offer moment-to-moment choices.	Create ambiguities that can be resolved through interpretive moves. Don't tell too much.
Variety	Don't repeat situations.	Continually develop the plot, characters, and themes. Don't belabor a point.
Consequence	Moves determine future situations.	Avoid gratuitous elements. Each beat should connect to the beats that follow it.
Predictability	The effects of moves can be anticipated.	Avoid plot holes. If you create expectations, follow up on them.
Uncertainty	Future situations are not inevitable.	Avoid clichés, stock characters, and formulaic situations. Outcomes should be uncertain.
Satisfaction	Desirable outcomes are attainable.	Avoid inconsistencies and loose ends. Satisfy coherence, expansion, and closure.

GAMES AS STORIES

The concept of interpretive play gives us a powerful tool for negotiating the overlap between game and story. Instead of treating gameplay and narrative as two independent systems that are uncomfortably yoked together, we can instead analyze them as two manifestations of a unified play process. The internal and external constraints that structure gameplay situations become constraints on story beats, and vice versa. Our role within the game becomes a character in the story, and the incidents within the story affect our moves within the game.

Such a ludonarrative convergence is not inevitable. It depends both upon the game being structured so that it invites interpretive play, and the player approaching the game with a motivation other than simply trying to win. The latter factor is particularly challenging, because the designer has no control over how the player plays. The emergence of interpretive play is contingent both upon the player's conceptual background and upon their willingness to pursue coherence, expansion, and closure as implicit goals within the game.

(Because of this, situational design is intended not only as a methodology for designing games, but also as a manifesto for playing them. The acknowledgement of the existence of these implicit goals gives us a way to re-conceptualize what we're doing when we play a game. Instead of being trapped within a game-centric system that ascribes significance to our moves only to the extent that they help us win, we can understand our moves within a broader player-centric system that accommodates a wider range of motivations. There are valid things to do with games besides trying to win them and those other things often can move and transform us in ways that winning cannot.)

While it is ultimately up to the player whether or not they explore narrative play, there are a number of things that a designer can do to facilitate it. The first is simply to provide stillness for it to unfold within. As with anticipatory play, interpretive play is non-interactive. It occurs in the mind of the player, and if the player is entirely absorbed by immediate moment-to-moment challenges, there will be no mental space left to engage with the narrative.

Similarly, the integration of interpretative play also needs to account for context switching. The constraints that govern our engagement with the narrative may overlap with our gameplay constraints, but they are not identical, so the transition between the two types of play must be handled gracefully. This is what underpins much of the hostility toward cut scenes in video games. The problem is not the narrative elements themselves, but rather the abrupt transition from one set of active constraints to another. We can't think about the story if we're still caught up in thinking about the game, even if thinking about the story is something we might want to do.

The transition between game and story needs to be cued with a clear threshold that signals the concomitant change in active constraints. But it also requires a smooth winding down of any anticipatory gameplay. A cut scene after a boss battle feels less jarring than a cut scene after a normal action sequence because boss battles themselves tend to be structured so as to shut down avenues of anticipatory play and steer the player toward closure.

The transition between game and story is also smoother when the two share active constraints. Story beats that directly reference the player's current gameplay context feel less jarring than ones that focus on entirely unrelated matters. For example, a story beat regarding an enemy's motivation works better if it comes at a moment when the player is already engaged in anticipatory gameplay to figure out how to beat that enemy. The placement of story beats within the overall experience shouldn't be haphazard, but rather should take into account the player's active constraints.

The corollary of this is that gameplay situations are themselves story beats. The moves that we perform to prevail within a gameplay situation also serve to define our role within the story. Explicit victory conditions can, in fact, drive narrative play by guiding us toward performative moves that we are then allowed to reflect upon in a following moment of stillness. So, for example, in a game like *Shadow of the Colossus*, we're given the explicit goal of killing a succession of giant bosses. The moves that we make during these boss battles are all directed toward accomplishing this goal. But in the aftermath of these battles there's a stillness that invites us to contemplate the significance of our actions. The queasy feeling of guilt that the game evokes arises from our attempts to make sense of the role that the game has lured us into performing.

The narrative power of performative moves can be even more profound if the situations that contain them don't offer much in the way of choice. If we don't have to work very hard to pick our next move, then we have space to consider the narrative significance of our moves as we're making them, instead of having to wait for a lull in the action to retroactively reflect upon them. Pressing the joystick forward to walk slowly toward our doom, tapping a button over and over to dig a comrade's grave, pulling a trigger to execute a helpless enemy—these sorts of moves work as powerful story beats precisely because they offer so little in the way of normal gameplay.

In fact, excessive interactivity can actually interfere with narrative play. If a game offers us a range of narrative moves (e.g., in a dialog tree) we may analyze the situation from a gameplay rather than a narrative perspective. Instead of playing with possible interpretations of the situation—trying to understand what's going on, or why the characters are doing what they're doing, or what the significance of it is—we may play to win. Instead of thinking about which move is more satisfying in narrative terms, we may think about which move grants us a gameplay advantage.

Often the most playful story beats are the ones that offer the player little external choice. Or, if there is an external choice, it's a choice that clearly has no impact on the game's explicit goals. In order to function as a story beat, a situation needs to offer narrative moves that satisfy our implicit goals. We need to be able to consider the implications of the situation for its own sake, not because it moves us closer to winning.

SUMMARY

Narrative play is similar to anticipatory play. Instead of making moves that change the external state of the game, we make moves that change our understanding of it. By treating narrative engagement as simply another form of play, we can understand how a game's story affects its gameplay and vice versa.

Narrative situations (or story beats) are structured by narrative constraints. These constraints are both textual and extratextual. They are the story elements that the game presents to the player, but also the player's own attitude and motivations. These attitudes and motivations are the product on their past engagement with other stories, but also their engagement with day to day life.

As we move from beat to beat within a story, we maintain a sense of where the story is headed and what it means. The repeated reformulation of this wandering anticipation is the main play that we experience within a narrative situation. However, if the story contradicts our expectations, we experience a crux. As with a gameplay crux, narrative cruxes are resolved through a rapid realignment of our internal constraints into a new interpretation of our circumstances.

Narrative situations obey the same heuristics as gameplay situations. In order for a story to engage us, it needs to offer us a succession of different interpretive choices. These choices need to have predictable consequences for our future narrative situations, but the course of the story should never become so obvious that we know exactly how it will play out. And finally, the narrative situations we encounter need to offer us the possibility of satisfaction through coherence, expansion, or closure.

The integration of narrative with gameplay requires us to negotiate the transition between different sets of active constraints. This can be facilitated by treating gameplay as a collection of performative moves. A game's explicit goals can be used to guide the player into such a performance. However, in order for narrative play to emerge, the demands of the game's explicit goals must be kept in check with intervals of either deliberate stillness, or low-consequence choices.

CHAPTER 8

Meaning

S EMIOTICS IS THE STUDY of meaning-making. It explores how objects and marks can be imbued with symbolic weight and used to transmit ideas between human beings. For example, it explains how an utterance like "hand me the screwdriver" relates to the act of a person handing another a screwdriver. Semiotics explains the connection between symbols and ideas, and how the transmission of ideas can emerge from the flow of symbols between speaker and listener.

The core concept of semiotics is the *sign*. Signs are the relation that exist between ideas and symbols, or, in semiotic terms, between signifieds and signifiers. So, for example, there is a sign that links the idea of a screwdriver with the word "screwdriver." This linkage is what allows communication to occur. If we want to ask or tell someone something about a screwdriver, we can use the sign to encode our thoughts with the word "screwdriver" and they can then decode the word by means of the same sign (Figure 8.1).

This model of meaning-making is fundamentally transactional and deterministic. It treats communication as something that flows from speaker to listener as a stream of signifiers. It's possible for such a communication to go awry (e.g., if I don't speak English—if you and I don't share the same signs—I may be baffled by the word "screwdriver") but there is no play in this system. There's no room for agency or creativity on the part of the listener.

While this model of communication works well for simple declarative utterances, it runs into trouble when we try to use it to understand how games make meaning. The problem is that much of the meaning we take away from playing a game comes not from the game telling us things, but

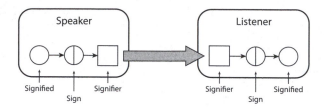

FIGURE 8.1   Semiotic coding and decoding.

rather from the game allowing us to do things. Meaning is not transmitted through a stream of signifiers, but rather evoked through a sequence of moves carried out within a system of constraints that is partially composed of our own motivations and attitudes.

This is not to say that the standard semiotic model is *never* useful for understanding how games tell us things. If we're playing a game and we come across a stop sign, we understand that the signifier we've just encountered should be decoded to mean "stop" and this understanding can be perfectly well explained through traditional semiotics. Games can communicate many things to us by presenting us with signifiers for us to decode. However, if we are going to understand how the moves we make within a game become meaningful, we need to step beyond the standard model. We need to construct a ludic semiotics, one in which meaning is not transmitted but constructed, and constructed in such a way that it takes into account both player agency and motivation.

THE LUDIC SIGN

Our reformulation of semiotics begins with a redefinition of the sign. The semiotic sign links an idea to a symbol. It describes a one-to-one mapping, or, alternatively, a procedure for coding and decoding. The idea of a screwdriver can be coded as the word "screwdriver" and then the word can then be decoded back into the idea again.

The *ludic sign* links a pattern to a constraint. A pattern is a feature of the world. It can be a word written on a page, or expressed as an audible vibration. It can be a daub of paint on a canvas, or an arrangement of pixels on a screen. And a constraint is, as previously defined, something that privileges one line of action over another.

If you're playing a first-person shooter and you see that you're approaching a wall, the pixels depicting the wall are the pattern, and your concomitant sense that you can't go that way is the constraint. The ludic sign describes the linkage that exists between our perceptions and the resulting mental system of bias toward particular lines of action that those perceptions evoke.

The ludic sign is similar to the semiotic sign. In semiotic terms, we'd say that the image of the wall is the signifier, and the idea that our way is blocked is the signified. With both types of sign, a feature of the external world is decoded as a particular idea in the mind of the player.

The primary difference between them is that the decoding of the ludic sign is merely the first step in our overall process of meaning-making. The meaning of a first-person shooter is not "there's a wall, there's a wall, there's a wall." The game's meaning is not transmitted directly through a sign-mediated encoding/decoding process. Rather, the sign-mediated encoding/decoding process contributes to the construction of a system of constraints, and it is within this system of constraints that meaning-making occurs.

In addition, the relationship that exists between pattern and constraint within the ludic sign isn't fixed. Standard semiotics depends upon a stable relationship between signifier and signified. In order for communication to occur, the sign that you use to encode "screwdriver" needs to match the sign that I use to decode it. But since the pattern in the ludic sign isn't transmitting meaning directly, it's not bound by the same limitation. You and I might have very different ideas of what a pattern represents, but depending on the play that unfolds within our respective systems of constraints, reliable communication between us can still occur.

Rather than being an entry in a shared codebook, the ludic sign is a description of an *event*. In this context, given this player, this particular pattern was translated into this particular constraint. The ludic sign encapsulates the translation of a perceived pattern into a constraint, but it is inherently fluid and slippery. We can never assign a fixed meaning to any pattern. We can only make normative assumptions about which constraints it's likely to evoke given the assumed circumstances of its perception and the assumed player who perceives it.

There are several consequences of this formulation of the sign. The first is that not all internal constraints are associated with corresponding patterns. It is possible for us to know things without having a word or symbol that refers to that knowledge. We experience these *ineffable constraints* all the time when we play games; we can feel what we should do, even though we find it difficult to articulate that feeling, or even think about it symbolically. Our decoding of a pattern may sometimes bring a new constraint into play, but other constraints can emerge from the cruxes we experience without a corresponding act of transmission.

Similarly, a pattern within a ludic sign doesn't need to correspond to any real-world entity; it's simply an arbitrary trigger for a particular collection of constraints. The word "unicorn" has the capacity to evoke a wide variety of constraints in the listener's mind, even though unicorns are imaginary. I can know lots of things about unicorns without ever seeing a real unicorn because knowing about unicorns is merely a matter of linking particular constraints to the pattern "unicorn." Or consider a word like "duty." I know what duty is, even though I can't see duty the way I can see a lamppost. Knowing the word "duty" gives me a way to tie together a wide variety of constraints that can't easily be triggered by an object or event in the real world.

Signs are a technology for the manipulation of internal constraints. Words and symbols give us a way to activate certain constraints, even if the real-world objects that those constraints are directed toward are absent. By saying "lamppost" I can get you to think about lampposts even though there isn't a lamppost present. Furthermore, signs allow us to construct collections of constraints that don't correlate with *any* real-world patterns; I can write a sentence like "Captain America always does his duty" and it will make sense to you, even though "Captain America" is a fictional character and "always" and "duty" are abstract concepts.

THE EPISTEMOLOGICAL CYCLE

We sometimes think of knowledge as a collection of facts. To this way of thinking, entities in the real world possess certain properties, and knowing about these entities is a matter inscribing these properties in our minds. So, for example, if I know that George Washington was the first president of the United States, that fact is inscribed in my mind like a sentence written in a book. Knowing is a matter of knowing what something *is*.

However, it's often more useful to think of knowledge not as a collection of facts, but as a collection of constraints. Knowing about something involves having a set of internal constraints that biases us toward particular courses of action. If I know that George Washington was the first president of the United States, I'm biased toward behaving in certain ways. For example, if you ask me who the first president of the United States was, I'm likely to say "George Washington." From this perspective, knowing isn't a matter of knowing what something *is*, but rather a matter of knowing what to *do*.

This may seem like a minor philosophical quibble, but it's actually a fundamental shift in how we perceive our relationship to the world. Our understanding of the world is not a matter of knowing what things *are*, it's a matter of knowing how they *behave*. We don't know that George Washington was the first president of the United States in an absolute, ontological sense. Rather, we know it in a functional, contingent sense. The world around us seems to unfold in a way that is in accord with George Washington having been the first president of the United States, so treating that fact as true is a useful constraint on our actions and expectations.

Believing that George Washington was the first president of the United States allows us to make accurate predictions about how the world around us will unfold. If we open a history book, there are certain words we expect to read. If we visit the U.S. capital there are certain sights that we expect to see. Our knowledge about George Washington is true, not because we've inscribed some fundamental feature of reality on our brains, but because we've adopted a constraint that allows us to make accurate predictions about the world around us. If we chose a different constraint (such as that Benjamin Franklin was the first president of the United States) our predictions will no longer be accurate.

If all of this seems similar to the model we constructed of anticipatory play, that's no accident. Anticipatory play is merely a special case of the general relation that exists between our minds and the world. This is the *epistemological cycle*—the foundational process that we use to make sense of reality. We know the world through a system of mental constraints. These constraints bias us toward particular lines of action and particular expectations about how the world will unfold. If our actions don't produce the desired outcome, or the world unfolds in ways we don't expect, we experience a crux and adjust our constraints to accommodate. (Figure 8.2)

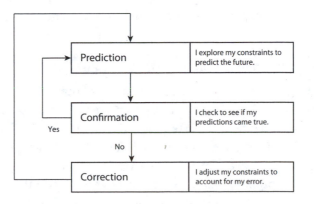

FIGURE 8.2   The epistemological cycle.

This way of thinking about knowledge is called pragmatism. Pragmatism is the philosophical view that it's impossible for us to know what the world is. All we can do is know how it behaves. Our beliefs about how the world behaves lead us to form predictions. And the deviations from those predictions lead us to adjust our beliefs to accommodate.

The epistemological cycle is continuous, unconscious, and fine-grained. We don't pause to try to consciously puzzle out the constraints that constitute our knowledge. We see a flash of red in our visual field, and within a fraction of a second we know that a sports car is headed toward us. The execution of the epistemological cycle is so rapid that we don't even register its existence. We see something unexpected and our brains instantly go to work to resolve the crux and settle on a new set of constraints to account for it. The flash of red becomes a sports car without us being aware of the elaborated process by which that knowledge was constructed.

The particular way that we correct our constraints in response to cruxes is a function of the epistemological cycle having to unfold in real time. Our brains don't try to resolve every crux by finding the *best* possible new set of constraints. They merely want to find *any* new set that's provisionally good enough to get the job done.

Our epistemological cycle is biased toward *parsimony*. When something unexpected happens we gravitate toward explanations that do the least amount of violence to our existing constraints. Making a minor tweak to one peripheral belief is much less time consuming than building up an entire new world view from scratch. So if we hear an unexpected noise at night, we're more likely to decide that it's the wind than that it's space aliens crawling on the roof. For most people, most of the time, the former explanation does much less violence to their existing constraints.

This same bias toward parsimony also encourages us to choose explanations that close off loose ends. Not only would "there are space aliens on the roof" require us to rework a large number of our existing constraints, it also generates more questions than it answers. Instead of just wondering, "What was that noise?" we're now confronted with, "Where did they come from?" and, "What do they want?" and, "Am I in danger?"

So we tend to resolve cruxes in ways that both close off loose ends and minimize disruption to our existing constraints. We do this because our epistemological cycle has to operate in real time. We can't reconsider everything we know about the world every time we hear an unexpected noise, and we also can't spend a long time exploring the extended rami- fications of an open-ended explanation. We always try to account for the unexpected within our existing system of constraints in the most parsi- monious way possible.

And this is why coherence and closure exist as implicit goals. It feels very satisfying to discover a move that preserves the coherence of a privi- leged set of constraints because such a move accommodates the parsimony of our epistemological cycle. By the same token, it feels very satisfying to discover a move that closes off ambiguities. When we manage to achieve both coherence and closure simultaneously it feels very satisfying indeed. We're encountering the unexpected, but we're smoothly able to integrate it into our existing system of constraints with a minimum of disruption and elaboration. We feel well-situated within the universe. The world is know- able, and we're capable of knowing it.

(The existence of expansion as a goal needs some additional explana- tion. We generally don't seek out situations that increase our uncertainty and that pose more questions that they answer. However, since play itself is pleasurable, we're willing to avoid closure in order to sustain it. In other words, we always have a tendency toward coherence and closure, even in non-playful situations, but expansion only becomes a goal while we're playing.)

Play is an idealized expression of our epistemological relation to the world. A game is an artificial arrangement of constraints that allows us to move smoothly through the epistemological cycle with just the right amount of friction. We don't play in order to learn. We play because we *can* learn. The pleasure of play is a side effect of the fundamental way that we go about making sense of the universe.

We can draw an analogy between games and parks. Parks are designed to replicate an idealized human habitat. They offer large expanses of grass to roam in, clumps of trees to provide shade and cover, and the reassuring trickle of fresh water. A park is the sort of spot our ancestors would have sought out on the African veldt. It's a good habitat for humans to survive in, and one in which we feel naturally comfortable in. If we'd evolved in a swamp, or a desert, or a forest, we'd have a different idea of what a park should be. A park is what we build when we want a place that makes us feel physically comfortable. And a game is what we build when we want a place that makes us feel epistemologically comfortable. Both parks and games have the particular properties they have because of the way that we as human beings exist within the world.

LUDIC SEMIOSIS

With our definition of the ludic sign, and our understanding of the epistemological cycle, we're now in a position to construct a model of ludic semiosis. This model is a general way of thinking about how communication operates, but one that is in particular well-suited to understanding how communication operates within a game. In other words, it's a model of communication that's designed to explain how the act of playing a game can result in meaning-making.

In ludic semiosis, both speaker and listener begin with an existing understanding of each other and of the context in which the communication is taking place. This existing understanding takes the form of a system of constraints. The speaker uses their understanding of the listener to continually make predictions about their future behavior and vice versa. This is true whether the speaker is attempting to communicate or not. I have a model of you that causes me to have certain expectations about you, and you have a similar model of me.

In order for me to communicate a message to you, I need to shift your internal constraints so that the message will emerge as a result. In order to accomplish this, I use my understanding of you to evaluate possible patterns until I find one that is likely to trigger the desired shift. When you perceive the pattern, you reverse the process. You run a simulation of me to determine what I probably meant by the pattern that I presented to you. The operation of your simulation produces a shift in your internal constraints that then generates the desired meaning as a result. (Figure 8.3)

We can break down the steps like this:

1. What should I say to get you to think of a dog?

2. The word "dog" should work.

3. Say "dog."

4. Why did he say "dog" to me?

5. He must want me to think about a dog!

6. You think about a dog.

This may seem very reductionist, but explicitly spelling out these steps is important if we're going to understand how the process works when the patterns and context become more ambiguous and slippery. However,

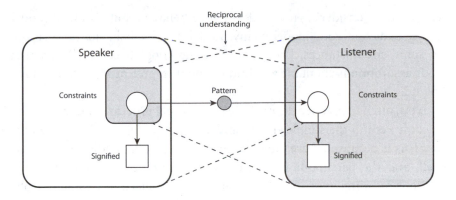

FIGURE 8.3   Ludic semiosis.

even in this reductionist form, the differences from normal semiosis are clear. The word "dog" doesn't encode the idea of a dog. It doesn't have a fixed meaning that we both agree upon. Rather, the pattern is a transient stimulus that emerges from our reciprocal understanding. It's what I think I need to say at the moment to produce the desired shift in your constraints. In a different context a different word might be needed, or a different shift might be triggered by "dog."

Because we don't share a common encoding—a common sign—reliable communication depends upon epistemological parsimony. It's not that I know that you will deterministically decode "dog" in a specific way. Rather, I know that you will probably shift your internal constraints in order to maintain coherence and closure. If we're walking down the street together and I say "dog" out of the blue, it's likely because I want to draw your attention to a nearby dog and your thoughts will converge on that interpretation.

But in other circumstances, other convergences may be possible. In other circumstances, you might decide that I'm saying "dog" to insult you, or to describe a costume, or as a pun. There are an infinite number of ways you can interpret a pattern, depending on your internal model of the speaker and your current circumstances. The parsimonies guide us toward likely interpretations, making communication possible, but don't guarantee certainty in encoding and decoding.

The steps we work through to encode and decode our utterances are complicated by the fact that our understanding of each other is not just reciprocal but also recursive. Within my model of you is a simple model of your model of me. And within that model of me is an even simpler model of you. So when I'm trying to settle on a pattern to communicate,

I'm not just considering my model of your behavior, but also your model of my behavior, your model of my model of your behavior, and so on. In some circumstances, I may avoid saying "dog" because I know that your assumptions about me will lead to you interpreting it in a way I don't intend.

Now, often in practice the recursive, reciprocal process of ludic semiosis is equivalent to the simple encoding/decoding model of standard semiosis. This is because we are often communicating to an audience we know well, and the parsimonious convergence of our utterances to a single, obvious meaning in the mind of the listener happens quickly and reliably. In these circumstances, our constraint-based encoding/decoding process resembles the fixed codebook of standard semiotics. "Dog" means dog and communication unfolds as though we shared a common collection of fixed signs.

Where ludic semiotics deviates from standard semiotics is how it handles situations where the listener's convergence on a meaning is nondeterministic. This is particularly true when the utterance itself is intended to be playful. After all, settling on a particular interpretation is equivalent to making a move with a system of constraints. If those constraints are arranged to satisfy the heuristics of play, then such an interpretive move will feel playful. The first heuristic says that for a situation to feel playful, picking a move needs to be nontrivial. So if an utterance is intended to be playful there won't be one single, obvious interpretation that we immediately snap to, but rather a collection of likely interpretations for us to explore. If we know immediately what the speaker means, we're not playing.

For example, consider puns. Puns are the simplest form of semiotic game. I say something that has several possible meanings, and your negotiation of the resulting ambiguity feels playful. The point of a pun is not to communicate a particular meaning as clearly as possible, but rather to structure a playful situation in the mind of the listener.

Of course, ambiguity is merely one of the heuristics of play. In order for a semiotic game to continue to feel playful over an extended period of time, it needs to take the other heuristics into account as well. So the constraints of an extended semiotic game need to generate a continually changing set of ambiguities. The way that we resolve one ambiguity needs to lead us to others. The different elements of the game need to hang together so we can understand how they relate to each other, but at the same time their connections shouldn't be so obvious that play is preempted. And finally, we need to have a sense that resolution is possible—that there is some satisfying interpretation that we can eventually converge upon.

Once we recognize the basic structure of semiotic games, it's easy to identify more of them. A semiotic game is a text that's intended to intersect with the internal constraints of an assumed player in such a way that it structures a series of playful situations. Within these playful situations, the player makes interpretive moves to work toward coherence and closure. The final configuration of their internal constraints as a result of these interpretive moves becomes the meaning ascribed to the game that initiated the experience.

The usual word we use to describe this sort of experience is "art."

Art is a type of text, but it doesn't transmit its messages to us directly. Rather, it offers a field of ambiguity and invites us to make interpretive moves in order to resolve it. The artist may have a particular interpretation in mind when they create their work, but, even taking parsimony into account, it's never certain that any player will arrive at the artist's interpretation, or even that different players will arrive at similar interpretations.

Art is necessarily autotelic; it exists as an end unto itself. It's an end unto itself because its primary object is the structuring of a playful encounter with a receptive audience. The more that art tries to be utilitarian, the more that it attempts to communicate something specific and direct, the more the interpretive moves we need to resolve it become obvious and dull, and the less playful it becomes.

All art functions like this. Novels, paintings, sculpture, music, dance— they all present themselves as a collection of patterns that evoke a set of constraints in the minds of their audience. These constraints invite a series of interpretive moves to resolve the challenges of coherence and closure. The enjoyment of engaging with art is the enjoyment of interpretive play. And the meaning that we take away from our encounter with such a work is the resulting shift in our internal constraints.

And this is why standard semiotics has a hard time grappling with the meaning of artworks. The meaning of a work of art is not transmitted, but constructed. The signifiers expressed by the words on the page of a novel, or the pigments on the canvas of a painting are not directly connected to what the work signifies. They are patterns intended to evoke playful constraints. And it is the play within those constraints that constructs the meaning that we take away from the experience.

HOW GAMES MAKE MEANING

Ludic semiosis provides the critical machinery we need to understand how games make meaning. The meaning of a game is not contained within the signifiers it transmits to the player. Neither is it is contained within the structure of the game's system of rules. Meaning consists of the strategies that the player invents in order to engage with the game. It consists of the accumulated shifts in their internal constraints that were triggered by playing. Meaning is the residue of experience. It is both embodied and contingent.

In a narrow technical sense, all games are meaningful because all games encourage us to develop strategies to help us play them. However, the meanings we take away from many games are self-referential. The strategies that we invent to play these games apply only to the game itself. So, for example, if we learn how to drift through curves in a racing game, that strategy can help us win the game when we play it, but it's not *portable*. It's not a strategy that applies to many situations outside of the game. It won't even be helpful when we drive a real-world car.

So when we talk about meaningful games, what we usually mean are games that change us in ways that matter *outside the context of their playing*. A game is meaningful if it leaves us with a lingering emotional resonance, or if it changes the way we think about the world or ourselves. This strategic shift occurs not within the ephemeral constraints we invent to cope with the game's passing challenges, but within the deep pre-existing constraints that we ourselves have brought to the experience. We're different for having played it, because we had to become different in order to navigate it.

The meaning of a game is never definite. It is always contingent upon what each player brings to the experience, and on the moment-to-moment choices they make as they navigate the game. The designer of a game may intend it to have a particular meaning, but the point of playing is not to puzzle out the designer's intent. The point of playing is to arrive at our own answers to the ambiguities that the game presents.

So, there is no single correct way to play a game. There is no single correct meaning that all players should try to extract. All ways of playing are valid, as are all the idiosyncratic personal meanings that players take away from the experience. So when we say, "this is what a game means," the unspoken caveat is always, "this is what a game means ... *to me.*" This is the meaning that I took away from my play experience.

However, the fact that the meanings we take away from games are idiosyncratic and personal does not mean that that they're not worth sharing and discussing. Players with similar backgrounds who approach a game with similar attitudes will often arrive at similar meanings. (In literary criticism terms, they are members of the same *interpretive community*.) The discovery that a game has affected another person in the same way that it affected you creates a powerful feeling of connection. And at the same time, the discovery that a game has affected another person in a profoundly different way can be a powerful moment of discovery. It's an intriguing crux. What amazing individual journey did they take to arrive at such an (apparently) perverse interpretation?

The fact that there's no single correct meaning for us to puzzle out does not mean that critical analysis of games is pointless. It just means that the point of critical analysis is not to uncover what a game "really means" or to figure out the "right way to play." All meanings are valid meanings, and all ways to play are the right way to play. Within the framework of situational design, our critical investigations are always descriptive, not prescriptive. They tell us *how* we made meaning with a game, not *which* meaning we should have made.

(Arguments over interpretation are always arguments over ideology. Defining what something "really means" is a way to establish which interpretive community is normative, and which other interpretive communities are outsiders. Now, if we step outside the narrow circle of play and consider the wider role that such play serves in society, we may decide that there are some interpretive communities that deserve marginalization. For example, a white supremacist interpretation of a game may be "wrong," not because it's an invalid way to play in and of itself, but because the constraints that allow such an interpretation to emerge are themselves odious. The notion that games don't have a single fixed meaning doesn't mean that the meanings we ascribe to them are pointless.)

If we want to create a game that lingers with players, there are several things we can do to make it more likely. The first is to rely as much as possible on the player's pre-existing constraints in the design of the game. We all have an innate sense of how the world around us operates, and meaningful games often co-opt that sense and then subtly subvert it.

For example, Brenda Romero's *Train* is a game about complicity. Mechanically, it's about transporting pawns in rail cars from one side of the board to the other. Thematically, it's about taking Jews to Nazi death camps. But what makes it meaningful is the way that it plays with our notions of "playing along." The rules to *Train* contain a number of gaps and omissions. In a normal game, being a good player means interpreting such gaps charitably. We try to "play along" in a way that will keep the game fun and friendly.

But the monstrousness of *Train's* theme means that the game doesn't deserve our charity. It's a game that deserves to be broken and ruined. Its power lies in how hard it actually is to take up the role of "bad player" and break the social contract and spoil the experience. *Train* takes our sense of how we should be in the world and puts us in a series of situations that undermine those comfortable internal constraints.

The playfulness of every game depends to some degree on the constraints that its players bring to the experience. A game is more likely to feel meaningful if it coaxes us into altering these pre-existing constraints. Meaningful games often work against the grain of our existing understanding of the world. They often feel uncomfortable to play, since they require us to shift our normal way of being in order to engage with them.

A second technique for making a game feel meaningful is to deemphasize winning. Since the win conditions of a game are part of the game's own self-contained system, working toward them can feel divorced from the world outside of the game. "Lighten up, it's only a game" is a common defense of troubling moves that threaten to break the closed circle of the play space. If winning is the only criteria for separating good moves from bad, then any move that helps you win is a good move and any move that doesn't is a bad one.

Emphasizing winning over coherence and closure can make a game more playful by establishing clear universal criteria for judging the value of a move. But paradoxically it can make it less meaningful because such moves then have little significance once the game is complete. Playing to win doesn't leave the same lingering traces as playing to satisfy our implicit goals.

For example, some of the most powerful moments in sport emerge when players set aside the drive to win at all costs and make moves that cohere with their principles of sportsmanship. The runner who gives up winning to help a fallen competitor, the gymnast who finishes his routine despite being injured, the team of underdogs who keep struggling even though they're certain to lose—these sorts of stories stick with us because they transcend the drive to win. The play in these situations breaks free of the limited axis of winning and losing and expresses something more powerful and universal.

So in designing games that are intended to be meaningful, give players things to do that lie outside the framework of winning. Give them moral decisions that have no in-game consequences. Give them ambiguous situations without a clear right answer. Give them puzzles that lead them to question the underlying premises of the game. Even when they're making decisions based on winning and losing, have these decisions also reinforce one of the implicit goals.

Think about the role that you are asking the player to perform. What strategies are you asking the player to adopt to navigate the game, and what are you training the player to do? Even a game with a clear win condition can feel meaningful if it guides the player into adopting a role that lingers with them afterward.

The game *Journey* is a cooperative platforming game. As you play you're randomly paired with another online player. You can't communicate with each other except with a single radar-like "ping." But when you're close to each other, your "glide meter" recharges faster. So as you play you quickly learn that staying close to your partner is a good strategy. It lets you jump farther and reach places you otherwise couldn't.

But this tendency toward companionship gradually becomes a habit, not just a strategy. You find yourself sticking with your partner even in situations where you don't need to jump, and even in situations where jumping is impossible. One of the meanings of *Journey* is this tendency toward companionship—the sense that on a hard journey we're better off if we stick together. The game doesn't tell us this. It invites us to perform it.

Finally, if you want a game to feel meaningful, provide space for introspection. If the player is constantly caught up in immediate play, there's no time to consider the significance of what they've done. After something significant happens, provide a space of stillness for the player to think about what just unfolded, and hopefully, what it means. *Shadow of the Colossus* acquires its power not just because it asks us to kill things that don't deserve to be killed, because it gives us a long, empty traversal afterward in which we can contemplate what we've done.

Games are a new art form, one whose full expressive capabilities are still in the process of being discovered. They have the capacity to deliver profound and deeply moving experiences. They are able to enmesh us bodily within an aesthetic experience in ways that other forms of art cannot. They have the ability to provide us with an explicit sense of agency and creativity—an awareness that the choices we're making and the meanings that we're creating both belong to us and flow from within us.

For games to live up to this expressive potential, we need to move beyond the notion that they are self-contained systems and incorporate the player into our designs. We need to move beyond the notion that the player is only playing when they are interacting. We need to move beyond the notion that games must be winnable. We need to embrace both stillness and aimlessness, and expand our conception of games to include both narrative and interpretive play.

Now, go make something amazing.

SUMMARY

Standard semiotics is based on the notion of the sign—a fixed linkage between signifier and signified that allows speaker and listener to encode and decode the utterances that pass between them. The ludic sign is an alternate formulation of this principle. The ludic sign links a pattern to a constraint. Rather than being shared between speaker and listener, it's embodied, transient, and contingent.

Our knowledge of the world is constructed through the epistemological cycle. We possess internal constraints that make predictions about how the world will unfold, and adjust these constraints when the world unfolds in unexpected ways. These adjustments obey the rules of parsimony: we try to minimize disruption to our constraints and close off future ambiguities. Ludic semiosis uses parsimony to achieve communication without speaker and listener possessing a shared sign. The speaker finds a pattern that will generate the desired constraints in their model of the listener. And the listener interprets the transmitted pattern according to their model of the speaker.

Meaning emerges from the operation of parsimonious convergence within the system of constraints in the mind of the listener. It's constructed, not transmitted. This is particularly true when the system of constraints obey the heuristics of play. Such a system allows the listener to engage in semiotic play. Meaning emerges from such play, but in a very nondeterministic way.

Games are made meaningful when the player's strategic constraints linger after the experience has ended. Meaning-making is more likely to occur when the affected constraints are part of the player's general sense of how the world works, when winning is de-emphasized, when the player is given a performative role, and when the game provides an interval of stillness in which semiotic play can unfold.

Index